Religion, Religious Groups and Migration

MIGRATION SERIES: 46

Religion, Religious Groups and Migration

Edited by Deniz Coşan Eke and Eric M. Trinka

Copyright © 2023 Transnational Press London

First published in 2023 by Transnational Press London in the United Kingdom, 13 Stamford Place, Sale, M33 3BT, UK.
www.tplondon.com

Transnational Press London® and the logo and its affiliated brands are registered trademarks.

Requests for permission to reproduce material from this work should be sent to: sales@tplondon.com

ISBN: 978-1-80135-120-1 (Paperback)
ISBN: 978-1-80135-121-8 (Digital)

Cover Design: Nihal Yazgan
Cover Photo by Pedro Lima on unsplash.com

Transnational Press London Ltd. is a company registered in England and Wales No. 8771684.

RELIGION
RELIGIOUS GROUPS
AND MIGRATION

Edited by

Deniz Coşan Eke and Eric M. Trinka

TRANSNATIONAL PRESS LONDON

2023

CONTENTS

ABOUT EDITORS

Deniz Coşan Eke (Dr. Phil.) works as a postdoctoral researcher in the Department of Alevi Theological Studies at the University of Vienna, Austria. She has been a visiting researcher on migration, religious groups, and interreligious dialogue at the University of Roskilde, the University of Westminster, and the University of Cambridge. She is the author of *The Changing Leadership Roles of Dedes in the Alevi Movement: Ethnographic Studies on Alevi Associations in Turkey and Germany from the 1990s to the Present* (Bielefeld, Germany: Transcript, 2021).

Eric M. Trinka (Ph.D.) is Assistant Professor of Religious Studies at Emory & Henry College in Emory, Virginia, USA. He is recognized globally as an expert on the formation and interpretation of religious texts in contexts of mobility. He is the author of *Cultures of Mobility, Migration, and Religion in Ancient Israel and Its World* (London: Routledge, 2022).

RELIGION, RELIGIOUS GROUPS AND MIGRATION

Deniz Coşan Eke and Eric M. Trinka

Introduction

The relationship between religion, religious groups, and migration is an important topic of recent social science debate. Migration affects all aspects of the lives of those who have left their homes, including facets characterized as religious. Religion and religious identity are linked to social, cultural, and political issues, including integration, identity negotiation, diasporic community formation, interreligious dialogue, and religious pluralism. On the one hand, migration can change religious cultures, rituals, and traditions through the experience of mobility and the response of the host country. On the other hand, religious groups can encourage migration. In this context, new forms of transnational interaction and organization have emerged that contribute to the reformulation of community and identity. In some cases, such changes can lead to new conflicts and even trigger religious radicalization.

This book is a collection of papers that brings together presentations on religion, religious groups, and migration from The Migration Conference. The aim is to empirically analyse discourses and practices of local, national, and transnational religious groups, along with the place of religion and migration in political, historical, cultural, and social transitions. The papers in this volume range in focus from micro to macro levels of analysis and investigate the roles of religion across various types of migration and displacement. The authors make use of a variety of approaches that include literature review, key-informant interviews, focus groups discussions, and textual analysis. Case studies of religious groups from various regional and historical contexts enhance the volume's methodological spectrum. The volume aims to provide both theoretical analysis and empirical evidence on the relationship between migrants and religion by using the concept of religion in its broader meaning, including:

a) religious stories, identities, and practices.

b) religious-based organizations and institutions, as well as interreligious initiatives.

c) religious-based discriminations, conflicts, and struggles.

The volume brings together academics and practitioners from a variety of contexts through interdisciplinary approaches and analyses of diverse religious landscapes present at different stages of the migration process. The contribution of this book is not only to help explore intersections, conflicts, and solidarity among religious groups, but also enrich our understanding of religious diversity, including its relationship to migration experiences.

Content and layout of the book

Christina Anne Kilby's contribution emphasizes examining the various intellectual resources that the Buddhist tradition offers to analyse causes of displacement, the responsibilities of sovereign governments, and the protection of displaced people. Kilby's work draws attention to a larger project initiated by the International Committee of the Red Cross and offers a critical-constructive approach to analysing Buddhist texts to explore the intersection between Buddhism and International Humanitarian Law.

In the second essay, Ehsan Sheikholharam discusses a crucial question often posed in relationship to "Muslim" immigrant's integration in Europe: "Is assimilation a prerequisite for socio-economic integration?" Bringing together studies of space and religious experience, Sheikholharam examines an urban renewal project in a Copenhagen neighbourhood to reveal the exclusionary nature of certain integration policies and the ways design shapes the concept of "other" in situations where immigrants are subject to discrimination.

Serdar S.Guner and Nukhet A. Sandal, the authors of the volume's third essay, bring the analytical tools of game theory to bear on the realities of informational asymmetry that often attend situations of interfaith dialogue in times of conflict. Although Güner and Sandal's work does not deal directly with contexts of migration, their findings on interfaith dialogue are broadly applicable to contexts of cultural contact where religious identity maintenance takes center stage, and where building participant buy-in is an important facet of succesful instances of interreligious dialogue.

The fourth essay, by Ece Cihan Erdem presents some of the ways children of Muslim immigrant communities connect with their cultural and religious heritage when living in a foreign country. Erdem's fieldwork data includes accounts of daily religious practice and analysis of discriminatory experiences towards Turkish parents and Muslim Sunni groups in Austria who send their children to Islamic courses in schools. Erdem argues that Islamic lessons help children understand and appreciate their Turkish and Muslim identities.

Deniz Coşan Eke explores the importance of the representation of religion, which plays a central role in the transmission of religious knowledge and traditions from generation to generation. In her study on the Alevi community in Austria to examine the rituals and group dynamics of the religious group in terms of its political, legal, socio-cultural dimensions Coşan Eke argues that each religious group includes intra-diversities and can be represented within a pluralistic approach.

The volume's sixth essay is devoted to researching harmonious integration between refugees, migrants, and local host communities in European countries after the "migration crisis" of 2015. Aleksandra Djuric Milovanovic and Amjad Mohamed-Saleem explore opportunities for immigrants to promote empathy, tolerance, and mutual understanding. This article draws attention to grassroots initiatives for religious dialogue and community building that intentionally target those occupying the middle ground in public migration debates. The essay also explores how policymakers might increase awareness of the potential role that faith-based organizations play in promoting social cohesion.

In the final essay, Eric M. Trinka engages the function of religious texts in contexts of mobility and migration. Focusing on Psalmodic literature, Trinka explores how Psalm 137 serves as both container and catalyst of collective memory in responses to traumatic movement.

"THE WORLD IS WITHOUT SHELTER, WITHOUT PROTECTOR": BUDDHISM, THE PROTECTION OF DISPLACED PEOPLE, AND INTERNATIONAL HUMANITARIAN LAW

Christina A. Kilby

Displacement is a common consequence of armed conflict that entails acute suffering and loss of protection. The prevention of displacement and the protection of displaced people are integral concerns of International Humanitarian Law (IHL), a universal body of law that seeks to limit the negative effects of war and to protect those who are not—or no longer—in the fight. To those ends, IHL includes provisions to prevent the unnecessary displacement of people and provides for the safety, shelter, health, hygiene, nutrition, and family unity of those displaced by conflict.[1] While refugees (those who cross international boundaries) fall under the legal protection of the 1951 Refugee Convention and the assistance of the United Nations Office of the High Commissioner for Refugees, internally displaced people (IDPs) move within the bounds of their state of citizenship or habitual residence. When that state is experiencing armed conflict, the government on which displaced people should normally rely for protection and assistance may be unable or unwilling to provide for their welfare. Furthermore, respect for the sovereignty of states can hinder international humanitarian intervention on behalf of IDPs. For this reason, IDPs are particularly vulnerable to prolonged suffering and *de facto* lack of protection during times of armed conflict, even though they are included in the provisions of IHL. The protection of IDPs during times of war remains a serious humanitarian challenge in every region of the world.

The United Nations Secretary-General recently appointed a high-level panel focused on internal displacement. Their report details the scale of internal displacement today as well as the complexity of factors that exacerbate the vulnerability of IDPs. At the end of 2020, an estimated 55

---

[1] Rules 129 and 130 from the International Committee of the Red Cross customary IHL study prohibit displacement of domestic or occupied populations, except when compelled by military necessity or by those populations' security. Rule 24 requires the removal of civilians from the vicinity of military objectives. Rules 131, 132, and 133 outline the requirements of protection and care for the displaced. International Committee for the Red Cross, "IHL Database: Customary IHL," accessed February 22, 2022, https://ihl-databases.icrc.org/customary-ihl/eng/docs/v1.

million people were internally displaced, with over 55% of them being children and youth.[2] Millions remain in situations of protracted displacement, often defined as displacement lasting three or five years, but in reality, often persisting to the second and third generations.[3] Conflict continues to be the largest driver of internal displacement, a fact that the high-level panel report attributes both to the continuing emergence of new conflicts and to an increase in average conflict length. Over the past twenty years, the number of people internally displaced by conflict has more than doubled and at the end of 2020 was at the highest number ever recorded (over 48 million).[4]

The objective of this chapter is to investigate several resources from the Buddhist tradition for analyzing the political ethics of protection for displaced people as well as the possible implications of those ethics for IHL. The United Nations Secretary-General panel's recommendations for addressing internal displacement include several items that can justify including Buddhism in IDP protection efforts. One recommendation from the panel is to "make solutions a nationally owned" priority.[5] From both legal and operational perspectives, states are critical actors in developing durable solutions to internal displacement. In many states in Asia, Buddhist traditions and values are integral to national identity and wield hefty influence in the policy arena. The contributions that Buddhism offers to the ethical challenges of internal displacement have the potential to impact governance (particularly in southeast Asia) and to improve the lives of IDPs in Buddhist-majority regions. Furthermore, the panel report emphasizes that "the whole of society" must be invested in solutions to internal displacement; this "whole of society" extends beyond the state to include civil society actors, such as religious leaders and religious organizations, who are sometimes overlooked in the secular humanitarian regime.[6]

While the Buddhist teachings are ultimately oriented toward the goal of transcending worldly existence, concerns about well-being and justice in this world and this lifetime are also strongly voiced across Buddhist traditions. Metaphors of displacement and refuge pervade the Buddhist teachings. "I take refuge in the Buddha, I take refuge in the dhamma, I

[2] United Nations Secretary-General's High-Level Panel on Internal Displacement, "Shining a Light on Internal Displacement: A Vision for the Future," (Geneva: United Nations Secretary-General's High-Level Panel on Internal Displacement, 2021), 2, https://www.internaldisplacement-panel.org.
[3] High-Level Panel, "Shining a Light," 3.
[4] High-Level Panel, "Shining a Light," 2.
[5] High-Level Panel, "Shining a Light," 13.
[6] High-Level Panel, "Shining a Light," 21.

take refuge in the sangha" is the first utterance of a Buddhist convert and a foundational commitment to follow the Buddhist path. This phrase is repeated day after day, in many languages, by lay Buddhists and monastics alike across the world. In the framework of Buddhist cosmology, all beings are refugees. From what do we flee? From the sufferings of cyclic existence, likened to a stormy sea that tosses us hither and thither and offers no stable ground on which to stand. This is *dukkha* (the first noble truth, usually translated as "suffering"): not only pain and loss, but flux, instability, and insecurity.[7] According to the Buddhist teachings, nothing in this world of conditioned and compounded things ultimately lasts, ultimately fulfills, ultimately relieves our restlessness. We are constantly on the move, from experience to experience and from birth to birth, seeking safety and stability but unable to find it anywhere in this ocean of changes. "The world is without shelter, without protector" reads the *Ratthapala Sutta*.[8] Only the dharma——the teaching of the Buddha——is an island in this sea, a place of haven and security. Because territorial security is always tied to political security, the metaphors of Buddhist cosmology appeal not only to a *place* of safety but to a *protector*: the Buddha is taught to be the great protector in whose care we can place our trust, the one who grants us refuge.

The most foundational metaphors in which the Buddhist tradition casts itself, then, are metaphors of displacement and refuge. This is no insignificant fact. We can infer from these metaphors that displacement was the most compelling human experience of insecurity at hand for the Buddha as he sought effective language for his teachings.[9] Displacement was widely known in the Buddha's world and it was a plight addressed with compassion and moral urgency in the Buddha's discourses as well as in early Buddhist narratives.

In the following pages, I employ a critical-constructive approach to analyzing several Buddhist texts in order to place the ethics of IDP protection in fruitful dialogue with the mandates of IHL. My research forms part of a larger project led by the International Committee of the Red Cross (ICRC), the global steward of IHL, exploring intersections between IHL and several of the world's religious traditions.[10] I joined the

---

[7] Kate Crosby, *Theravada Buddhism: Continuity, Diversity, Identity* (Oxford: Blackwell-Wiley, 2014), 17.

[8] "Ratthapala Sutta: About Ratthapala" (MN 82), translated by Thanissaro Bhikkhu (*Access to Insight*, 2013), http://www.accesstoinsight.org/tipitaka/mn/mn.082.than.html.

[9] Buddhists generally believe that the Buddha was a perfect teacher who could convey his teachings in exactly the right language for each listener.

[10] International Committee of the Red Cross, "Religion and Humanitarian Principles," accessed February 22, 2022, https://blogs.icrc.org/religion-humanitarianprinciples/.

ICRC's work on Buddhism and IHL in order to enhance the understanding and implementation of IHL in Buddhist communities and to share Buddhist insights into suffering, protection, and humanitarianism with the wider global community.[11] Involved in this project are academic researchers, Buddhist monks and nuns, Buddhist lay practitioners and community leaders, military and government officials, legal practitioners, and humanitarian practitioners. The project's goal is not only to extend the reach of IHL, but also to enrich and challenge IHL with insights from religious and cultural traditions like Buddhism, traditions that constitute humanity's earliest and most powerful sources of humanitarian principles. The ICRC's work thus far has engaged scholars and practitioners of Islam, Hinduism, Buddhism, Christianity, Sikhism, Aztec traditions, Mayan traditions, and Indian tribal traditions to cultivate dialogue about humanitarian principles and to develop non-western frameworks for articulating these universal principles.

Displacement, Morality, and Law

Since 2011, a steep increase in displacement has been well documented by the United Nations.[12] During this time, anti-refugee rhetoric in some resettlement countries—in particular, the United States and Australia—has come to conflate the plight of displaced people with moral depravity. The invocation of religious scriptures to argue for the moral standing of refugees has often sparked theological statements to the contrary. For example, former U.S. president Donald Trump's adviser Paula White famously argued, "I think so many people have taken biblical scriptures out of context on this, to say stuff like, 'Well, Jesus was a refugee.' Yes, He did live in Egypt for three-and-a-half years. But it was not illegal. If He had broken the law then He would have been sinful and He would not have been our Messiah."[13] For White, and for many others, to be a refugee is to break laws, and to break laws is inherently immoral. There are factual problems with White's statement, notably her ignorance of the fact that refugees are recognized under international law not as illegal migrants but as a legally protected group. (A second problem with her statement is her theological assumption that breaking a law is

---

[11] International Committee of the Red Cross, "Religion and Humanitarian Principles: Buddhist Circles," accessed February 22, 2022, https://blogs.icrc.org/religion-humanitarianprinciples/category/buddhist-circles/.

[12] United Nations High Commissioner for Refugees, "Figures at a Glance," accessed February 22, 2022, https://www.unhcr.org/en-us/figures-at-a-glance.html.

[13] "Paula White Faces Theological Backlash After Saying Jesus Never Broke the Law," *Sojourners, July 11, 2018*, https://sojo.net/articles/paula-white-faces-theological-backlash-after-saying-jesus-never-broke-law.

inherently immoral, when according to Christian tradition, Jesus broke laws frequently yet was sinless, but I leave that problem to the Christian theologians.) Despite the misunderstandings undergirding her statement, White's reflexive association of displacement with immorality has been shared by many in the Anglo world. She is right about something, though: displacement, law, and morality are bound up together.

Buddhist sources, varied as they are, present a different and compelling articulation of the relationship between the plight of the displaced on the one hand and law and morality on the other. Admittedly, displacement is not a topic that has been systematically addressed in Buddhist sources the way it has been in international law; my argument here draws on Buddhist texts whose primary aims and audiences differ from mine. Still, according to Buddhist tradition, the word of the Buddha is "oceanic" in scope, "immeasurable" in meaning.[14] Just as religious commentators do, scholars continue to mine new layers of wisdom in old words. To begin understanding how Buddhist traditions address the relationship of displacement to law and morality, I turn to several narratives from the Buddhist *jātakas*, a tradition of stories of the previous lifetimes of the Buddha in which he develops the spiritual capacities that will eventually lead to his enlightenment as a man named Gotama. The *jātakas* are sometimes called fables because they offer lessons about key Buddhist virtues, but the *jātakas* offer much more moral instruction than meets the eye. As narratives, full of flawed characters and set in particular contexts, these texts build worlds of ethical possibility in which the relationships between past actions and present challenges are intricately illustrated. Both hopeful and tragic dimensions of human agency play out in these stories as the future Buddha interacts with kings and servant maidens, animals and gods, merchants and thieves. In my readings of these *jātakas*, I attend not only to the virtues they extol, but also to the ethical horizons to which they gesture,[15] asking how those horizons might inform the possibilities before our global community now in addressing internal displacement during times of war.

The Reluctant Tortoise: A Buddhist Mandate to Migrate

In the Pāli scriptures, which form the textual canon venerated by Theravāda Buddhists, there is a story about one of the Buddha's past lives

[14] Maria Heim, *Voice of the Buddha: Buddhaghosa on the Immeasurable Words* (New York: Oxford University Press, 2018), 33-59.
[15] Hallisey and Hansen, "Narrative, Sub-Ethics, and the Moral Life: Some Evidence from Theravāda Buddhism" *Journal of Religious Ethics* 24, No. 2 (1996): 305-327.

when he was a potter.[16] He lived near a river. In years of flood, the river would overflow to fill a nearby lake. In years of drought, the lake would dry up. The story goes that the fish and turtles always knew when a drought year was imminent, so in those years they would swim from the lake back into the river before the water in the lake dried up. One year, however, there was a reluctant tortoise who loved his home in the little lake so much that he refused to swim to the river. He thought to himself, "here I was born, and here I have grown up, and here is my parents' home. Leave it I cannot!"[17]

When all the water in his little lake dried up, the tortoise buried himself deep in the clay. One day the future Buddha, the potter, came to harvest clay and struck the poor tortoise with his spade, splaying open his shell and mortally wounding him. As the tortoise lay in the mud dying, he cried out,

> "Here was I born, and here I lived; my refuge was the clay; And now the clay has played me false in a most grievous way; Thee, thee I call, oh Bhaggava [Blessed One]; hear what I have to say!
>
> Go where thou canst find happiness, where'er the place may be; Forest or village, there the wise both home and birthplace see; Go where there's life; nor stay at home for death to master thee."[18]

In the *jātaka* narratives, we rarely encounter the future Buddha killing anyone. Indeed, the premise of the *jātaka* collection is that the future Buddha is busily perfecting himself in virtue and wisdom. Yet without any knowledge of the tortoise's situation or any intention to do him harm, the Buddha nonetheless kills the poor tortoise. This narrative is set within the horizons of a tragic moral world, one in which even without ill intent, each of us will inevitably harm another. One being's livelihood impinges on another's. There is no one in particular at fault for the tragic outcome of the story, and just as the future Buddha is not blamed for killing the tortoise, the tortoise is not blamed for the drought conditions that make his home unsafe. At this point in our reading, the story exhibits a morally neutral posture toward displacement, a neutrality that is rendered in part by the neutral character of the natural environment. No ill intent is attributed here to the conditions that render the tortoise's home unsafe.

---

[16] "Kacchapa-Jātaka," Translated by W. H. D. Rouse in *The Jataka; or, Stories of the Buddha's Former Births*, Volume 2, Edited by E.B. Cowell (Cambridge: Cambridge University Press, 1895), accessed on February 22, 2022, https://onlinebooks.library.upenn.edu/webbin/metabook?id=jataka. Story no. 178, 55-56.
[17] "Kacchapa-Jātaka," 55.
[18] "Kacchapa-Jātaka," 56.

They just happen.

Yet while the tortoise is not blamed for needing to migrate, he *is* blamed in the text for failing to do so. He refuses to accept the situation around him, to use the information at his disposal, and to make the necessary move to ensure his survival. The potter, the Buddha-to-be, imputes a moral dimension to the tortoise's reluctance: this tortoise is too attached to his home, the place where he was born, where he grew up, and where his parents lived. In Buddhist doctrine, attachment (Pāli *taṇhā*, often glossed as "desire," "clinging," or "thirst") is the root cause of suffering and the engine that drives this cyclic existence of births and deaths. Attachment does not only include the most egregious expressions of greed or exploitation, but also includes the most subtle and seemingly innocuous ways in which we crave things that are ultimately not fulfilling and depend upon things that are not ultimately dependable. These attachments, which are rooted in fundamental ignorance about the way things are, lead to suffering whereas non-attachment leads to the end of suffering. The exemplars of non-attachment in the Pāli scriptures are monastics, the members of the Buddhist community who have chosen to renounce their homes and take up the homeless life in order more fully to practice the Buddhist teachings. To be an ordained monk or nun is frequently glossed as "going forth from home into homelessness" because renouncing attachment to one's home is such a significant sacrifice, a foundation for all the other forms of renunciation that monastics undertake.

The tale of the reluctant tortoise is presented in a narrative frame that further illuminates and deepens its instructive potential for contemporary displacement challenges. The Buddha narrates this story to a young man who had experienced an outbreak of disease in his family. At his parents' direction, he had escaped from their home through a hole in the wall and fled to safety, then returned later (presumably, after his family had all succumbed to the disease) to dig up the buried fortune that the family had saved. His willingness to flee danger saved his life and even "restored the family fortunes," as his parents had hoped, and so when he met the Buddha he was healthy and prosperous, in the perfect position to learn from the Buddha to offer him material support.[19]

In this narrative frame, disease functions as a natural consequence of compounded existence, much like the flood and drought in the tortoise's

---

[19] "Kacchapa-Jātaka," 55.

story. There is no fault in experiencing the horrors of illness, but there is virtue in the willingness to sacrifice one's home for the sake of life. Interestingly, this framing narrative introduces a resonance with the IHL provisions (rules 132 and 133 in the IHL study) for the rights of the displaced to voluntary return to their homes when conditions are safe enough, and for the rights of the displaced to maintain their claim on their private property.[20] The moral of the story seems to be that there is merit not only in the preservation of life, but also in the preservation of displaced people's family property, which can then contribute toward more rapid self-sufficiency for those affected by displacement and even enable them to support community institutions.

In this *jātaka*, to migrate when one's survival is threatened is likened to the renunciation of monastics——the "wise" among us——who seek life (ultimately, *nirvana*), who "find happiness" wherever there is life, and who can feel equally at home in "forest or village." This parallel may sit uneasily with today's reader because there is a degree of choice and privilege involved in monastic renunciation that is not present in contexts of displacement due to disaster, disease, or conflict. These two examples of homelessness are not equivalent. Instead, they address the virtues of wisdom and non-attachment at two different ends of a scale that spans the immanent on one hand and then transcendent on the other. The use of a story of immediate, this-worldly displacement in order to illustrate the urgency and sacrifice with which monastics are encouraged to seek nirvana only works, as a literary device, if both examples are taken seriously on their own terms.

Just as monks and nuns give up their homes in order to seek spiritual security, sometimes humans or other animals must give up our homes in order to seek physical security. Both examples are forms of the wisdom that sees a situation for what it is and values life and liberation more than attachment to home or tradition. Unlike the contemporary rhetoric in which migrants who are fleeing for their lives are not only criminalized, but are even described as morally evil, in this Buddhist narrative the willingness to leave one's home for the sake of one's life is upheld as a moral virtue and a sign of wisdom. To be so attached to home that one would risk death is both foolish and tragic because this life, this "precious human birth" as Buddhists call it, is an enormous gift and opportunity to be cherished. Because Buddhism is a tradition that prizes detachment, this scriptural narrative portrays displaced people, those who are willing

---

[20] International Committee of the Red Cross, "IHL Database: Customary IHL."

to "go where there is life," as moral exemplars.

The lessons that the tortoise offers in this *jātaka* can also instruct the communities that host displaced people. Excessive attachment to home and culture can quickly turn to exclusion, xenophobia, or nationalism, so that displaced people are denied a place of safety. The wisdom—and compassion—that values life more than home can inspire host communities or resettlement states to receive displaced people even at the cost of change in their local socio-cultural fabric. (Unfortunately, the community's role in protecting the displaced is not as visible in the *jātaka* stories as the king's role, which I explore below.)

The Buddhist mandate to "go where there is life" joins similar mandates from the Abrahamic religious traditions. The Hebrew patriarchs Adam, Abraham, Lot, Jonah, Jacob, and Moses all migrated when either God or safety called them to do so. Building on the experience of the Hebrew prophets, the *Quran* indicates that able Muslims have a duty to seek safety in another land when they are oppressed. Surah 4:97 asks, "Was not the earth of God spacious enough for you to flee for refuge?" To fail to migrate in cases of oppression is understood to deny the graciousness of God and the capaciousness of his earth, and therefore to earn God's censure. A similar mandate to migrate can be drawn from the provision in the Hebrew *Torah* of *pikuach nefesh,* the "primacy of life," which teaches that even a commandment from God must be broken if it endangers human life.[21] Life is the good that all laws must serve.

The *jātaka* narrative of the reluctant tortoise offers one point in a larger constellation of Buddhist scriptural perspectives on displacement: that to flee home for the sake of life is not a moral failing, but a sign of moral wisdom and non-attachment. The relationship between displacement and morality is defined positively in this story, although law is not specifically addressed here. Other *jātakas* offer perspectives on the moral dimension of governance and displacement, one of which I consider now.

---

[21] Maimonides derived this interpretation from Leviticus 18:5, "You shall therefore keep my statutes and my rules; if a person does them, he shall live by them: I am the LORD." See Asher Lopatin, "Pikuach Nefesh: The Jewish Value of Saving a Life," My Jewish Learning, accessed on February 22, 2022, https://www.myjewishlearning.com/article/pikuach-nefesh-the-overriding-jewish-value-of-human-life/.

The Dream (or Nightmare) of a King: Displacement and Poor Governance

In another *jātaka* from the Pāli scriptures, King Pasenadi of Kosala experiences a series of troubling dreams whose portents he cannot understand.[22] At his wife's advice, he asks the Buddha to interpret them for him. Each of his sixteen dreams centers on a dark omen that bespeaks calamity for kings of the future as the morality of kings wanes. The dreams richly portray ancient ideals about what constitutes a flourishing or a declining society. As Pasenadi recounts from his ninth dream,

> "I saw a deep pool with sloping banks overgrown with lotuses. From all directions, a wide variety of animals came to drink water from that pool. Strangely, the deep water in the middle was terribly muddy, but the water at the edges, where all those thirsty creatures had descended into the pool, was unaccountably clear and sparkling. This was my ninth dream. What does it mean?"

> [The Buddha replied:] "This dream too will not come to pass until the future, when kings grow increasingly corrupt. Ruling according to their own whim and pleasure, they will never make judgments according to what is right. Being greedy, they will grow fat on lucrative bribes. Never showing mercy or compassion to their subjects, they will be fierce and cruel. These kings will amass wealth by crushing their subjects like stalks of sugar cane in a mill and by taxing them to the last penny. Unable to pay the oppressive taxes, the citizens will abandon their villages, towns, and cities, and will flee like refugees to the borders. The heart of the country will be a wilderness, while the remote areas along the borders will teem with people. The country will be just like the pool, muddy in the middle and clear at the edges."[23]

This text makes no bones about the fact that the king's immoral conduct is the direct cause of his subjects' displacement (in this case, akin to "internal displacement," although this text was composed before the advent of modern states defined by boundaries of sovereignty). The subjects have been forced to "flee to the borders, like refugees" in order to escape the oppressive governance that makes life in the center untenable. Although armed conflict is not mentioned in this tale, here we

---

[22] *Jātaka Tales of the Buddha: An Anthology,* Translated by Ken and Visakha Kawasaki (Kandy, Sri Lanka: Buddhist Publication Society, 2009), vol. 1., 141-150.
[23] *Jātaka Tales of the Buddha,* 146.

encounter a classic case of internally displaced people who do not enjoy the protection and security they deserve from their government.

In this dream, the traditional Indian mandala of governance is inverted. In Indian tradition, in which Buddhism began and remains deeply rooted, a mandala is a three-dimensional diagram of political organization that is structured like a palace: a circular tower surrounded by a square with four doorways to the four directions. The most powerful figure resides in the center with attendants organized around the periphery. The mandala has been used as an organizing principle for governance (for example, in some periods in premodern India, a territory of rule might be called a "*mandala*") and also in religious rituals, where hierarchies of spiritual beings are invoked and arrayed spatially, from center to periphery. The various lineages of tantric Buddhism frequently employ the ritual construction, visualization, and consecration of mandalas.

Here, the application of mandalas to political organization is most relevant. Whereas a king should serve as the powerful and virtuous center of his mandala, from whom righteousness and well-being emanate in expanding circles, in King Pasenadi's nightmare the center of the kingdom is a place of suffering and depravity while his subjects flee to the periphery. The mandala is inverted, which is a sign of civilizational collapse. When the king fails to serve as the moral anchor for his mandala, everything falls apart and people scatter to the edges of his power.

The Buddhist (and Hindu) doctrine of karma directly links the morality of a ruler to that ruler's power and sovereignty. Only by establishing roots of virtue can the karmic fruits of political success manifest. One of the chief ethical duties of the king, as outlined in classical Indian tradition, is to protect those without a protector, to give "the gift of fearlessness," as the tradition frames it.[24] The gift of fearlessness is the gift of refuge——the gift of life——for refugees, prisoners, animals destined for slaughter, or any being whose life is threatened. The gift of fearlessness is also "the gift that kings give when they ensure that their subjects live in security," a statement that emphasizes preventive as well as reactive modes of protection.[25] In Indian tradition, even a king's use of military force is understood as a

---

[24] Christina Kilby, "The Global Refugee Crisis and the Gift of Fearlessness," *Journal of Buddhist Ethics* 26 (2019): 307-327.
[25] Maria Hibbets, "Saving Them from Yourself: An Inquiry into the South Asian Gift of Fearlessness," *Journal of Religious Ethics* 27, no. 3 (1999): 441.

method for ensuring the protection of his people, which is his duty. Expounding upon the gift of fearlessness, the *Laws of Manu* from Hindu tradition claim that "those who give fearlessness receive, in turn, sovereignty."[26] The king who protects those under his care is the only one endowed with the power to rule. Furthermore, he enjoys power over a flourishing kingdom, while the king who oppresses those under his care sees his power and his kingdom crumble from the center.

This second *jātaka* narrative, when considered in the context of Indian traditions of political organization and the ethics of governance, affirms the moral responsibilities of those in power to care for those who find themselves displaced and without protection. Prevention of displacement by "ensur[ing] that their subjects live in security" as well as protection of the displaced, when displacement must occur, is kings' moral duty as well as a pragmatic necessity for maintaining a stable society. Consequently, a displacement crisis reflects badly not on the moral character of those fleeing their homes, but on the moral character of their leaders who have the power to create conditions of safety but fail to do so. Here, displacement, morality, and law are bound together in the conduct of the king or state. Displacement is a sign that the law (or the conduct of the king) has failed morally; a moral state, on the other hand, draws people toward a center of security rather than impelling flight to the borders.

One challenging horizon that the *jātakas* often present is that the ethical possibilities available to someone in the present are tied to the stores of merit that person has accumulated in the past. In the *jātakas*, kings might miraculously avert war by meditation or give away all their kingdom's wealth without causing the collapse of the economy. These unlikely scenarios—in which extreme renunciation of state violence or state wealth yield worldly success—are not plausible models for today's states, who must make difficult decisions about military action or economic policy. These surprising outcomes can only, it appears, be attributed to karma. Righteous kings in these stories must have accumulated much merit in the past to meet with the conditions in which their virtuous conduct could yield such results. All this is little consolation for contemporary states, or non-state armed groups, who may be mired in deeply complex and intractable conflicts where the karmic conditions for non-violent or virtuous resolutions are not apparent. Are one's possibilities for virtuous rule, for protecting the protectorless and offering security to one's people, so severely limited by one's moral

---

[26] Hibbets, "Saving Them from Yourself," 442.

actions in the past?

Not One Drop of Blood: The Power of International Support

A third *jātaka* for consideration here assumes an ethical horizon in which a king is not alone in his struggle to rule righteously. When he chooses to exercise virtue, allies come to his aid. The story "Not One Drop of Blood" narrates that there is a righteous king of Kasi named Maha-Silava who is known for his clemency and generosity. Refusing to retaliate against enemies, he gives bags of gold to ruffians who make trouble in his kingdom because, when asked why they behaved badly, they claim that they needed money and were not able to make a living.[27] King Maha-Silava's reputation for leniency and weakness inspires the king of Kosala to attack Kasi. True to character, King Maha-Silava declares, "Not one drop of blood shall be shed because of me. Let those who covet my kingdom take it. You must not fight."[28]

The invading king buries Maha-Silava and his army up to their necks and leaves them for the jackals. With wit and perseverance, Maha-Silava bites a jackal, wiggles free, and liberates the rest of his army. A helpful demon (*yakkha*) magically brings him his robes and sword and transports him to the royal chamber where the invader from Kosala is sleeping. Still refusing to attack his enemy, King Maha-Silava smacks him on the belly with the flat of his sword. When the king of Kosala awakens, he is full of shame, admitting that

> "Even those fierce *yakkhas*, who feast on the flesh of corpses, knew your worth, but I, a human being, could not appreciate your goodness. Now, at last, I understand, and I vow never again to plot against anyone who possesses such singular virtues as you do. Please forgive me," he begged, as he prostrated himself at King Maha-Silava's feet. "Forgive my wickedness, and let us be friends as long as we live." As a token of his sincerity, he insisted that King Maha-Silava lie down on the royal bed while he himself stretched out on a couch nearby.

At dawn, King Kosala ordered a drum to assemble his army in front of the palace. Standing before his men, the king praised King Maha-Silava, formally returned his kingdom to him, and, in the presence of his entire force, again asked the king's forgiveness.

---

[27] *Jātaka Tales of the Buddha*, vol. 1, 119-124.
[28] *Jātaka Tales of the Buddha*, vol 1., 121.

"From now on," he promised King Maha-Silava, "while you rule your kingdom, I will keep watch to protect you. It will be my duty to deal with rebels."[29]

King Maha-Silava's compelling virtue and self-restraint (when he could have easily killed his enemy) earn him a lifelong ally. The reader may dismiss this unlikely ending by attributing it to good karma; only extreme stores of merit could make possible a situation in which a king flourishes by renouncing violence and engaging in lavish generosity. Importantly, though, this story does not make any explicit appeals to karma. It is King Maha-Silava's virtuous conduct in the present that inspires a rival king to become his protector.

While many of the karmic trajectories explicitly traced (or implicitly assumed) in the *jātakas* are individually focused, this story opens a wider horizon of ethical possibility of collective action. One's own past karma is not the only determinant that makes possible the miracle of restraining state violence[30] while simultaneously enjoying worldly success. International humanitarian law is predicated on humanitarian principles shared across every human society, and the ICRC provides a global organizational framework for states and other organizations to work together to implement those principles and to provide humanitarian protection during times of armed conflict. Allies matter.

The contributions of partners and allies (whether the ICRC, states, or other organizations) to one state's humanitarian needs can take many forms. The high-level panel on internal displacement discussed above agrees that "harnessing international financing" in order to share the burden of protection of IDPs is an important way to increase protection.[31] States who share borders with one another may also productively partner in addressing displacement crises in border regions. Finally, states and non-state armed groups who have traditionally shared a Buddhist heritage may challenge each other to uphold foundational Buddhist ethics in their conduct, even during times of armed conflict.

From a Buddhist perspective, we might consider IHL as a manifestation of the good karma of our global community, karma that one state or group may draw upon when its own situation is immensely challenging. It is a blessing, a fruition of merit, that states have agreed to

---

[29] Jātaka Tales of the Buddha, vol. 1, 124.
[30] IHL does not concern the prevention of war, but rather the exercise of precaution and restraint within the conduct of war.
[31] High-Level Panel, "Shining a Light," 33.

a legal framework that facilitates the delivery of humanitarian relief to civilians and provides protections for displaced people during armed conflicts. While on the one hand our interdependent existence (according to Buddhist doctrine) has tragic dimensions, such as our inevitable harm of one another even without ill intent, our interdependence also makes possible our ability to aid one another substantially in times of distress and to influence one another with regard to political ethics and humanitarian values. It is not only possible, but to the benefit of all involved, that states aid each other in fulfilling their humanitarian duties during times of conflict, especially in the case of displacement. Good governance and humanitarian assistance can serve to decrease refugee flows to neighboring states and support regional stability with future benefits that reach beyond a single state.

The Causes of Displacement

Displacement figures in two of the three *jātakas* considered above. The cause of displacement in the story of the reluctant tortoise, had he heeded it, is a change in the natural environment. The natural environment is another character in this tragic moral world, a character who—without any ill intent—causes suffering and death for its animal inhabitants as the waters rise and recede from the lake. Talking tortoise aside, the *jātaka* tale is quite realistic: in a world of *dukkha,* a world of impermanence and interdependence, the very structure of things involves suffering. In the Pāli scriptures, climate and floods are frequent sources of suffering, as are fires, elephant tramplings, disease, and other natural occurrences. Displacement due to natural disaster or degradation is an inevitable part of life, fully recognized in the scriptural canon.

The cause of displacement in the story of King Pasenadi's dreams is immoral governance. Moral and immoral kings are frequent characters in the *jātakas*. In the lifetime of the Buddha Gotama, advising kings was a common form of service to humankind. The Buddha, born into a royal family himself and destined for a kingship that he renounced, understood how significant an effect governance has upon the well-being or misery of all living beings. Poor governance and unrestrained armed conflict continue to be major drivers of displacement, but they can be ameliorated with advising, state reforms, and external support and accountability.

In our modern context, displacement due to conflict and poor governance is deeply interwoven with climate displacement. Although the concept of a "climate refugee" has not been legally defined, the reality of displacement due to climate degradation, whether within or across state borders, is well recognized. As the global climate continues to warm and become more volatile, a sharp increase in climate refugees is predicted (up to 143 million IDPs by 2050).[32] Climate change is also predicted to precipitate further conflicts as geopolitical tensions are heightened by the scarcity of clean water and other factors.[33] Furthermore, many countries already enduring conflict or its aftermath have been identified as increasingly vulnerable to the effects of climate change, including Afghanistan, Bangladesh, and many countries in sub-Saharan Africa.[34] In sum, there is no longer an ultimate separation between conflict-induced displacement and climate displacement; reducing internal displacement during times of armed conflict will ultimately require attention beyond the scope of IHL to address climate change and to support environmental sustainability efforts.

Intersections with International Humanitarian Law

International humanitarian law, or IHL, is codified in the Geneva Conventions of 1949, the Additional Protocols of 1977, and other international treaties and conventions that "seek, for humanitarian reasons, to limit the effects of armed conflict."[35] These rules are known colloquially as "the laws of war "or "the laws of armed conflict," and they include provisions such as protection of non-combatants, humane treatment of prisoners of war, and restrictions on the means of warfare (for example, prohibiting the use of landmines). Whereas international human rights law applies in peacetime, "many of its provisions may be suspended during an armed conflict."[36] IHL, on the other hand, applies during times of armed conflict, whether international in scope or domestic (legally, the term is "non-international armed conflicts"). Because IHL applies within state borders during times of conflict, and because conflict is one of the major causes of displacement globally, IHL is a highly relevant legal instrument for protecting IDPs.

[32] Kanta Kumari Rigaud et al. "Groundswell: Preparing for Internal Climate Migration," World Bank, Washington, DC: 2018, accessed on February 22, 2022, https://openknowledge.worldbank.org/handle/10986/29461

[33] Department of Defense, Office of the Undersecretary of Defense (Acquisition and Sustainment), United States of America, "Department of Defense Draft Climate Adaptation Plan," Report Submitted to National Climate Task Force and Federal Chief Sustainability Officer (1 September 2021), 13.

[34] Notre Dame Global Adaptation Initiative. "ND-GAIN Country Index," accessed on February 22, 2022, https://gain.nd.edu/our-work/country-index/rankings/.

[35] International Committee of the Red Cross, "What is IHL?," accessed on February 22, 2022, https://www.icrc.org/en/doc/assets/files/other/ what_is_ihl.pdf.

[36] International Committee of the Red Cross, "What is IHL?"

The global steward of IHL is the International Committee of the Red Cross. Recognizing that international humanitarian principles are deeply rooted in the world's religious traditions, and that "religious communities have been carrying out humanitarian action for far longer than other humanitarian actors" have, the ICRC has for years now been engaged in collaborations with religious scholars, practitioners, and leaders to explore the intersections between IHL and religious traditions.[37] Their aim is to build "more effective humanitarian coordination and partnerships" that are attentive to cultural context and that are enhanced by the immense resources that religious institutions and networks offer.[38]

As a scholar of Buddhism, I am currently working with the ICRC on their Buddhist Circles initiative with a focus on internal displacement. IHL includes several provisions for displaced people. First, IHL prohibits displacing a population "unless the security of the civilians involved or imperative military reasons so demand" (Customary Rule 129).[39] Second, IHL prohibits "deport[ing] or transfer[ring] parts of their own civilian population into a territory they occupy," or otherwise using displacement to alter the demographic composition of an occupied territory (Customary Rule 130). Third, IHL requires that displaced persons "are received under satisfactory conditions of shelter, hygiene, health, safety and nutrition and that members of the same family are not separated" (Customary Rule 131). Fourth, IHL assures that "displaced persons have a right to voluntary return in safety to their homes or places of habitual residence as soon as the reasons for their displacement cease to exist" (Customary Rule 132). Finally, IHL protects the property rights of the displaced (Customary Rule 133).

There are many fruitful avenues for debate about whether it can be acceptable, from a Buddhist point of view, to engage in war at all.[40] IHL is not a body of law designed to assess whether the cause of a war is just or unjust (*jus ad bellum*), but rather a body of law designed to promote justice in the conduct of war (*jus in bello*). When we accept the human reality that wars do occur, in Buddhist contexts as elsewhere, we can observe that the logic of power inherent in IHL is strikingly similar to that of ethical governance in the Indian sources examined above. IHL rests upon the claim that if a state (or non-state armed group) is powerful

---

[37] International Committee of the Red Cross. "Religion and Humanitarian Principles."
[38] International Committee of the Red Cross. "Religion and Humanitarian Principles."
[39] International Committee of the Red Cross, "IHL Database: Customary IHL."
[40] See the forthcoming special issue of *Contemporary Buddhism* (2022) on Buddhism and International Humanitarian Law.

enough to take up arms, then it is powerful enough to assume responsibility for the protection of those who are not, or no longer, in the fight. To conduct war at all is to be responsible for conducting that war in a way that upholds humanitarian principles as the international community has agreed upon them.

My readings of the Buddhist *jātakas* above echo the high-level panel report's calls for mutual support and burden sharing. In my view, the fullest and most universal implementation of IHL depends upon the mutual support and resources that are available to states or non-state armed groups who are engaged in conflict. The responsibilities to uphold humanitarian principles in war are coupled not only with legal accountability for the parties to a conflict, but also with a call to action for the international community, embodied particularly in the work of the International Committee of the Red Cross but extending to other states and actors as well, to assist in supporting and implementing those principles.

The Buddhist narratives examined above illuminate another aspect of IHL that has not been widely considered: its forward-looking orientation. Even though IHL is primarily focused upon the immediate situation of conflict, many of its wise provisions lay the groundwork for a just and functioning society after conflict ends. When enemy prisoners are treated humanely, there is better hope of reconciliation and reintegration after the conflict ends. When civilian property and means of livelihood are protected, there is better hope that the economy can rebound after the conflict ends. When natural resources are protected, there is better hope that the land and its resources will regenerate after the conflict ends. When children are protected, there is better hope that the next generation may rise up to do better than the last.

In terms of karma, IHL is a wise framework of laws that makes possible the fruition of virtue and justice in the future. The more that the principles of justice and humanity can govern the conduct of war, the more realistic dream a society's flourishing becomes for the future. In King Pasenadi's dream, the terrors of an oppressive and crumbling kingdom lie far in the future——far enough that there is still ample time to change the ending of the story.

References

Crosby, Kate. *Theravada Buddhism: Continuity, Diversity, Identity.* Oxford: Blackwell-Wiley, 2014.

Department of Defense, Office of the Undersecretary of Defense (Acquisition and Sustainment), United States of America. "Department of Defense Draft Climate Adaptation Plan." Report Submitted to National Climate Task Force and Federal Chief Sustainability Officer. 1 September 2021.

Hallisey, C. and A. Hansen. "Narrative, Sub-Ethics, and the Moral Life: Some Evidence from Theravāda Buddhism." *Journal of Religious Ethics* 24, No. 2 (1996): 305-327.

Heim, Maria. Voice of the Buddha: Buddhaghosa on the Immeasurable Words. New York: Oxford University Press, 2018.

Hibbets, Maria. "Saving Them from Yourself: An Inquiry into the South Asian Gift of Fearlessness," *Journal of Religious Ethics* 27, no. 3 (1999): 435-462.

International Committee of the Red Cross, "Religion and Humanitarian Principles: Buddhist Circles," accessed February 22, 2022, https://blogs.icrc.org/religion-humanitarianprinciples/category/buddhist-circles/.

International Committee of the Red Cross. "IHL Database: Customary IHL." Accessed February 22, 2022. https://ihl-databases.icrc.org/customary-ihl/eng/docs/v1.

International Committee of the Red Cross. "Religion and Humanitarian Principles." Accessed February 22, 2022. https://blogs.icrc.org/religion-humanitarian principles/.

International Committee of the Red Cross. "What is IHL?" Accessed on February 22, 2022. https://www.icrc.org/en/doc/assets/files/other/ what_is_ihl.pdf.

Jātaka Tales of the Buddha: An Anthology. Translated by Ken and Visakha Kawasaki. Kandy, Sri Lanka: Buddhist Publication Society, 2009.

"Kacchapa-Jātaka." Translated by W. H. D. Rouse in *The Jataka; or, Stories of the Buddha's Former Births*, Volume 2. Edited by E.B. Cowell. Cambridge: Cambridge University Press, 1895. Accessed on February 22, 2022. https://onlinebooks.library.upenn.edu /webbin/metabook?id=jataka. Story no. 178.

Kilby, Christina. "The Global Refugee Crisis and the Gift of Fearlessness." *Journal of Buddhist Ethics* 26 (2019): 307-327.

Lopatin, Asher. "Pikuach Nefesh: The Jewish Value of Saving a Life." My Jewish Learning. Accessed on February 22, 2022. https://www.myjewishlearning.com/ article/pikuach-nefesh-the-overriding-jewish-value-of-human-life/.

Notre Dame Global Adaptation Initiative. "ND-GAIN Country Index." Accessed on February 22, 2022. https://gain.nd.edu/our-work/country-index/rankings/.

"Paula White Faces Theological Backlash After Saying Jesus Never Broke the Law." *Sojourners*. July 11, 2018. https://sojo.net/articles/paula-white-faces-theological-backlash-after-saying-jesus-never-broke-law.

"Ratthapala Sutta: About Ratthapala" (MN 82). Translated by Thanissaro Bhikkhu. *Access to Insight*, 2013. http://www.accesstoinsight.org/tipitaka/mn/mn.082.than. html.

Rigaud, Kanta Kumari, Alex de Sherbinin, Bryan Jones, Jonas Bergmann; Viviane Clement, Kayly Ober, Jacob Schewe, Susana Adamo, Brent McCusker, Silke Heuser, Amelia Midgley. "Groundswell: Preparing for Internal Climate Migration." World Bank. Washington, DC, 2018. Accessed on February 22, 2022. https://open knowledge. worldbank.org/handle /10986/29461.

United Nations High Commissioner for Refugees. "Figures at a Glance." Accessed February 22, 2022. https://www.unhcr.org/en-us/figures-at-a-glance.html.

United Nations Secretary-General's High-Level Panel on Internal Displacement.

"Shining a Light on Internal Displacement: A Vision for the Future." Geneva: United Nations Secretary-General's High-Level Panel on Internal Displacement, 2021. https://www.internaldisplacement-panel.org.

BORDERS WITHIN BORDERS: SUPERKILEN AS THE SITE OF ASSIMILATION

Ehsan Sheikholharam[1]

From Cartoons Controversy to Public Park

Debates surrounding immigration in Europe often justify anti-Muslim policies through the discourse of failed integration and "culture wars" (Roy, 2020: 105). This failure is epitomized by the proliferation of isolated neighborhoods in European metropolises. Predominantly non-white immigrant communities close themselves off from the rest of society, creating internal borders within cities (Lapeyronnie & Courtois, 2008). These "ghettoized" spaces, then, become the target for radical groups and fundamentalist ideologies. To explain this phenomenon, often referred to as "community withdrawal," political discourse points the finger at religion. The inhabitants of these spaces are said to be unwilling to embrace societal norms, which in turn precludes their capacity to integrate into mainstream society. The reason for this unwillingness—as the logic of this xenophobic justification goes—is that the religion of immigrants is incompatible with secular and liberal values. Thus, to be socially and economically integrated, Muslim immigrants should first be culturally assimilated.

While some programs such as preschool education of "ghetto children" are explicit about their agenda of cultural assimilation (Barry & Sorensen, 2018), state-sponsored architectural projects can transform identities without exposing their cultural aims. This paper examines the design of Superkilen park, a public space that was devised to address marginality in a working-class neighborhood in Copenhagen, Denmark. One of the reasons that the Municipality commissioned the project was the social unrest following the cartoons controversy (Steiner, 2014; Akšamija, 2016). Before analyzing the park, I will highlight the

[1] Ehsan Sheikholharam, University of North Carolina - Chapel Hill, United States.
E-mail: ehsansh@live.unc.edu
Acknowledgement: This is a reprint of the article which appeared originally in International Journal of Religion: Sheikholharam, E. (2022). Borders within Borders: Superkilen as the Site of Assimilation, International Journal of Religion, Vol.3, No.2, pp.121-137. DOI: https://doi.org/10.33182/ijor.v3i2. 2290. Grateful for the permission granted by IJOR.

significance of the latter for debates on cultural assimilation of Muslims in Europe.

In response to the terrorist attack on the Charlie Hebdo office in January 2015, the secular West as well as Muslims across the world used the slogan, *Je suis Charlie*, to express solidarity with the victims (Klausen, 2009). The cartoons controversy, however, did not start then and there: some of the drawings were reprints of what had already been published ten years earlier by a Danish newspaper, *Jyllands-Posten*. The cartoons—satirical representations of the Prophet Mohammad—triggered waves of protest. Yet as the work of Jytte Klausen shows, not only were the reasons for these protests more complicated, but only a few amounted to violence. The publication of the "original" drawings in 2005 was not the first battle over representations of Muslim embodiments either. A year before *Jyllands-Posten* issued the cartoons in Denmark, the French government had decided to ban veils along with other (conspicuous) signs of religion from public schools. The decision was the culmination of fifteen years of legal and political dissent that started in Gabriel Havez middle school in Creil, France, when, in October 1989, three schoolgirls refused to remove their headscarves in the classroom (Scott, 2010). This incident, *L'affaire du foulard,* was a decisive moment in which explicit hostilities towards Muslim bodies turned into a political debate. Significantly, this event was already colored by Ayatollah Khomeini's notorious *fatwa* against Salman Rushdi in 1989, ten years after the Islamic Revolution of Iran. What appeared as a menace to the West was not simply that the Revolution heralded the official establishment of Islamic fundamentalism, as Bruce Lawrence (1989) argues, but that political Islam was in search of new forms of cultural representations (Roy, 1994). The headscarves became a warning sign for fundamentalist ideologies—reminiscent of Khomeini's imposition of the veil on Iranian women.

More than struggles against the ideology of Political Islam, these events (cartoons and veils) are two cases of Europe's unease with public religion and Muslim embodiments in particular. The cartoons aimed to provoke a distressed minority to a stage of agitation, and thereby prove within their reactions the following claim: Danish Muslims are not "truly" Danes because they are not tolerant of critique of religion. Jyllands-Posten's cartoons were not merely about blasphemy—breaking a taboo through satirical representations of the Prophet. Rather, the twelve drawings enumerated many reasons why Muslims do not belong to the secular West: inequality of sexes, Bedouin and primitive culture (hence, an uncivilized civilization), and intolerance toward criticism. The reproduction of the cartoons in France did not merely change the geography of the same debate. By being reproduced in a different context and deriving a similar affective response, it framed the struggle not as *national* but as *civilizational*. It was no longer the cultural norms of this or that group of Muslim immigrants that could not fit into this or that national identity. The point was to demonstrate that (a) Islam is an alien civilization to the Judeo-Christian traditions, and (b). Muslims do not belong to the geoculture of secular Europe. The headscarf controversy was predicated on a similar premise. Those French Muslims who condemned the ban could not appreciate the fact that French secularism meant the retreat of religion from the public sphere.

Unlike Denmark that recognizes the Evangelical-Lutheran Church as the official religion of the State, France has a unique history of anti-clerical secularization.[2] Marcel Gauchet (2015) shows how since the French Revolution attempts at pushing religion to the private sphere were marked by a series of legal battles: 1795, cutting the salary of all recognized cults; 1801 (*régime concordataire*), cutting the link between the Catholic Church and the Monarchy; 1905, the separation of the church and the state; and 1946, when France become officially *République laïque* and *laïcité* became an integral part of the Constitution. The same subtractive secularization was at work in public education, where the law of 1882 (*les lois Jules Ferry*), disentangled classrooms from religious education (Ozouf, 1982).

Already more than a century ago, an educational system hostile to religion and a public space intolerant of religious signs were institutionalized. It does not come as a surprise that anticlerical satire in France is a political tradition is as old as the Revolution itself. The question remains if Denmark also shares a similar history of hostility towards religion? Incidentally, it was "revealed that a few years earlier Jyllands-Posten had refused to publish defamatory cartoons portraying

---

[2] Immediately after the 1789 Revolution, wearing a cassock (soutane) was banned outside of religious ceremonies. The Law of 1905—which declared the official separation of the Church and the state—reopened the debates on religious clothing. The rationale behind the law was
the following. Not only will the presence of such representations provoke conflict between lay (Protestant) citizens and (Catholic) clergy, but it also institutes social hierarchy within the society at large by giving the clergy a higher status. Finally, it perpetuates a regime of privilege among the clergy themselves, demanding submission to religious authority. In short, wearing of soutanes should be banned because it disturbs the social order, as conceived by the state.

Jesus on the grounds that the images would offend readers" (Klausen, 2009: 87). In further justifying the refusal, the editor claimed that the drawings "will provoke an outcry."

In analyzing the cartoons controversy, many have focused on questions of blasphemy, tolerance-intolerance, and limits of the secular critique (Asad et al., 2013). Others have interrogated its implications for the role of the State in disciplining its less-desirable subjects (Badiou, 2017, Todd, 2015). What has not been adequately examined is the role of space in debates on integration. What is the link between the lived experiences of immigrants, their housing conditions, and the kind of discontent that resurfaced in the cartoons riots?

The Nørrebro neighborhood was one of the areas that exhibited riots and other incidents of conflict with the police attributed to the cartoons. To address social unrest and the "ongoing ghettoization of the neighborhood," the Municipality of Copenhagen devised an urban design project (Akšamija, 2016). An important element of this large-scale initiative was the realization of the Superkilen park.

Soon after its completion in 2011, the park received sweeping accolades. Most remarkably, it received the 2016 Aga Khan Award for Architecture since it promoted "integration across lines of ethnicity, religion and culture" (*Superkilen, Aga Khan Development Network*, n.d.).

Participatory Design

The site of the project was a leftover space resulting from the removal of tramway tracks that circumnavigated the inner-city for roughly a century—1880s to 1972 (*For 40 År Siden Kørte Sidste Sporvogn i Danmark*, 2012). This derelict land was haunted by delinquency, drug trafficking, and the underground market. Through a closed competition, the Municipality commissioned a design coalition comprised of architects (Bjarke Ingels Group), landscape designers (Topotek 1), and artists (Superflex).[3] They turned the space into a theme park by dividing the linear stretch of land into three color-coded zones, each dedicated to distinct programmatic activities. The theme for Red Square is "market/culture/sport;" the Black Market is a spatial metaphor for "urban living room;" and the Green Park is dedicated to

---

[3] As Brett Bloom explains, the Municipality involved some of the citizens from the area in selecting the design coalition.

"sport/play." To substantiate these themes, each zone is "populated by a curated selection of iconic urban furniture" (Akšamija, 2016).

The design partners—who are often commissioned to tackle urban problems through design solutions—customized a community engagement technique for the park. Instead of representing Danish elements, "Participation Extreme aimed at incorporating diverse objects from geographies familiar to (non-national) inhabitants of the neighborhood. Individuals of the surrounding housing blocks were invited to share what they wished to be incorporated into the park. The idea was that if immigrants could see something familiar in the space of their daily experience, social isolation would be replaced with a sense of belonging. Barbara Steiner, whose publication on the park includes interviews with the design partners, refers to these objects as "agents of integration" (2014: 25). The objects, she argued, "create relationships with different people and [...] establish emotional connectivity." Martin Rein-Cano, the main landscape designer from Topotek 1, pointed to the fact that while immigrants can bring with them small tokens, they cannot have their urban scenes, streetscapes, and monuments.

To facilitate integration, therefore, the design grafted elements of immigrants' former visual-scape onto the landscape of their daily experience. "In the end," said Rasmus Nielsen from SUPERFLEX, "the park is this mesh-up, gigantic Tivoli, with a big emphasis on telling stories about each object" (Steiner, 2014: 31). The principal architect of the project, Bjarke Ingels, touted that the team "would not need to design anything;" all they needed to do was to "let people recommend cool stuff from all over the world" (Steiner, 2014: 25). The designers' description of the park is saturated with terms such as cool, fun, playful, etc. Designed through this method, Superkilen does not resemble what one might expect from a community park. The design is a composition of "108 objects and 11 trees," populating a wedge-shaped space. The undulated ground is primarily built of colored asphalt and is adorned by strips of white lines. The lines themselves meander to accommodate variegated urban furniture. Instead of typical elements such as trees, plants, and flowers, the landscape is fashioned with light posts similar to those of the Las Vegas strip as well as idiosyncratic play equipment. What type of urban landscape is this and who would want such a park? Already in the late 1960s, Denise Scott Brown and Robert Venturi suggested that it is more sensible to represent the function of a building through signage, "decorated shed," instead of turning the volume/form into an expression, "duck" (1972). But what would a signage "mean" or "signify" in a park that does not have an explicit programmatic function compared to a building?

The neighborhood for which the park was designed accommodates the largest percentage of immigrants in Denmark (Larsen & Möller, 2013). To emphasis the multinational character of Nørrebro, the design team created a colorful tapestry of 60 national flags, allegedly corresponding to the nationalities of the residents of the neighborhood. One can notice within this colorful map flags of the US, Canada, England, and Italy, not to mention the USSR. What is remarkable about this image is that it represents all nations on the same level, with no order or hierarchy (all flags are the same size and scattered without any particular order). Yet, as Alfred Korzybski (1933) cautioned us, there always exists a minimal gap between representations (map) and the experience itself (territory). One should therefore be suspicious of the dissimulating potential of this "map" that inscribes differences within a radically egalitarian order.

Image 1. View of the "Black Market" zone (photo credit: Scott D. Haddow)

Mapping of the Neighborhood

To understand what is hidden behind this egalitarian façade of public participation, it is enough to look at the land use and the zoning map of the district. The area hosts the largest concentration of Islamic centers in Denmark. This is not a surprise because "more than half of" the immigrants in the neighborhood come from Muslim majority countries (Larsen & Möller, 2013). Near 11,000 "Muslim" residents of Nørrebro are from "Bosnia Herzegovina, Turkey, Somalia, Morocco, Iran, Iraq, Jordan, Lebanon, Pakistan and Syria." Why did the official discourse surrounding the design shy away from talking about Muslims as the main reason for this project?

As part of the comprehensive plan, the Municipality had conducted a spatial study for the district of Nørrebro. The report reflected on the dynamics between "immigrants and ethnic Danes" focusing on the issues related to "[r]ecognition, redistribution, multiculturalism, [and] positive selectivism" (Larsen & Möller, 2013: 19). Yet these studies did not make it clear who among these 60 nationalities needed recognition. Does this lacuna pertain to Muslims who would be offended to learn that they have been officially flagged as the problem, or is it meant to protect the Municipality from accusations of xenophobia and Islamophobia?

Unlike the public narrative that refrained from pointing the finger at the "Muslim" constituency, the expert (design) discourse was explicit about it. For example, the on-site review commissioned by the Aga Khan Award explains how the project was "informed by the riots and vandalism in the area linked to the so-called cartoons controversy" (Akšamija, 2016: 24). The report further notes: "In Nørrebro, the cartoon controversy sparked a number of riots, vandalism, flag burning and violent incidents involving clashes between the police and frustrated Muslim youth who were throwing stones and Molotov cocktails." The report then zooms back and positions the design within the larger frame of cultural integration: "Although the presence of Muslims and/or representation of Islam in the West were not the primary reasons for the inception of this larger urban renewal project", argued Azra Akšamija, "the issue of integration and the coexistence of different immigrant cultures was on the top of priority for this plan and the subsequent the competition brief for Superkilen."

The designers themselves used less-polished language in talking about the park. The sense of resentment was conspicuous in the neighborhood, said Bjarke Ingels, "and people in Denmark were suffering a bit from the ambiguity of *being tolerant* [emphasis added]" (Steiner, 2014: 70). It is precisely this narrative gap that interests me: Superkilen as a project for celebration of diversity and pluralism, or a project for assimilation of a group who can barely be tolerated.

A Curious Object

In Superkilen, idiosyncratic objects are juxtaposed, but it is not clear if and how they should relate to each other. For example, in the Red Square, three signs mounted on light posts strike as symbols of Communism, seemingly representing brands from the USSR, Cuba, and (Mao-era) China. Being aware of the provocation, the brochure of objects, "Superkilen's 108 Objects and their History," released by Superflex (2012), claims that "the red aspects" do not refer to "Soviet communism" (p. 20). The explanation goes further to suggest that the red has never been red: "The Russian word 'krasnaya', which today primarily means red, used to mean 'beautiful'." This ambivalence is not confined to the relationship *between* objects; individual objects, too, exhibit unresolved tensions. While there are several objects with intriguing stories, I will focus on a neon lamp that stands tall at the center of the main space. The shape appears to be a replica of the symbolism of star and crescent. Yet, the star is replaced by a tooth.

The brochure describes the sign as a largescale re-production of a dental clinic sign from Doha, Qatar. Yet the detailed story of the crescent, especially how they "found" this object, was never explained. In an architectural festival in Ukraine, however, the landscape designer shares the trajectory of the object (Martin Rein-Cano, 2017). An immigrant from Muscat, who during door-to-door inquiry was asked to share something of his home country, comes back with a pile of photos. Flipping through pictures, *the designers* pulled out this curious image. The sign, interestingly, did not belong to the tenant but his aunt who had paid for his migration to Denmark. The name on the sign, Vasantha-Sena Devarajan, hints at an Indian pedigree. To advertise her business, Doctor Sena appropriated a symbol that she recognized as culturally significant to her "Arab/Middle Eastern/Muslim" clients. Perhaps this was already a capitalist mode of consumption of the sacred.

Image 2. Dental clinic signage in Doha, Qatar (right), and its replica in Superkilen

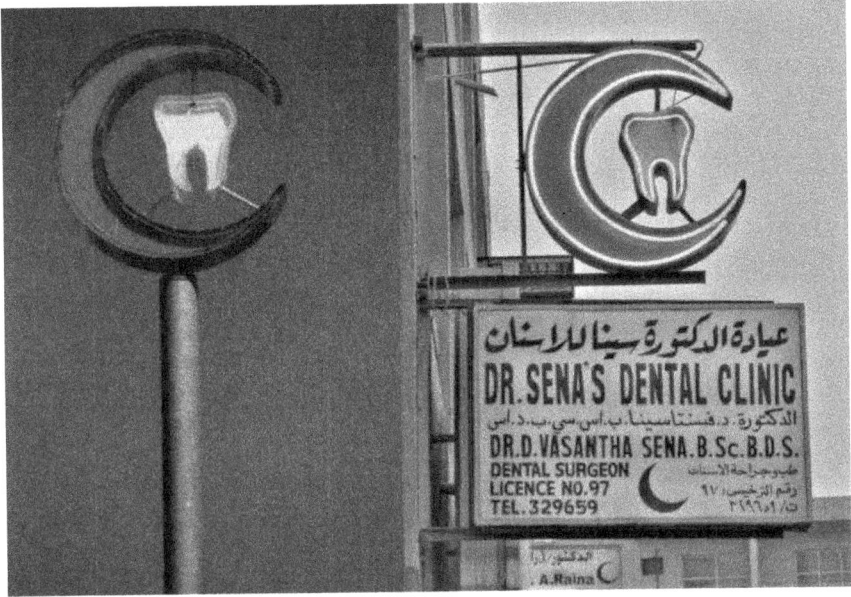

What is intriguing about the design does not concern its aesthetics *per se*, but the ways in which symbols have been transformed from one historical, cultural, and geographical context to another. It is precisely through this trans-positioning (or deterritorialization, if you wish) that symbols formerly associated with the sacred are turned into profane signs.

This "democratization" goes beyond material remix. The designers trace an expanded genealogy of the crescent-moon to undermine its cultural significance for Muslims. The above-mentioned brochure argues that "the crescent moon is one of the world's oldest religious symbols and not something exclusive to Islam" (Superflex: 12). The symbolism of crescent, it continues, dates "back to 2000 years BC when the moon used to be the symbol of the Mesopotamian god, Sin." To extend the emphasis on the pagan origins of crescent to its accompanying star, the paragraph goes on to claim that in ancient mythology the star was "usually representing Sin's daughter Ishtar, goddess of war, love, and sex." Thus, instead of signifying the political power of the Ottoman Empire, the sign is really about sex, sin, and love. Nancy Fraser and Alex Honneth (2006: 1) articulate this penchant for this postmodern and playful remixing of cultural horizons as follows:

"Hegel's old figure of 'the struggle for recognition' finds new purchase as a rapidly globalizing capitalism accelerates transcultural contacts, fracturing interpretative schemata, pluralizing value horizons, and politicizing identities and differences." Conversely, the author of the Aga Khan report regards this playful refashioning of symbols in crescent-tooth as a "positive dimension of cultural diversity," and believes that it has been done "in a respectful manner" (Akšamija, 2016: 24). This hybrid sign, she argued, will undermine stereotypes about Muslims' intolerance toward religious symbols.

Image 3. Crescent and tooth, and crescent and star

When in September 2005, Jyllands-Posten published a cartoon of the Prophet with crescent as the contour of his face and star as an eye, the Muslim world perceived it as a blasphemous insult. Here, the landscape provides a decentered semantic field where symbols are inserted within an entirely invented regime of signification. The crescent-tooth does not mean the same as crescent-star, regardless of the fact that the former references the latter.

The otherwise blasphemous sign functions as a vaccine of sorts—a low dose of trigger that does not amount to violence. This seemingly humorous play is intended to desensitize Muslims, to dismantle the "moods and motivations" that give symbols "an aura of factuality," as Geertz (1993: 87-125) would have said.

Today, identities are supposed to be open and pluralist. For those at social and economic margins, expectations to reinvent their identities are ceaseless. But, to what extent can cultural identities be expanded, remixed, and democratized? For historians, cultures have always been in flux—grafting, borrowing, mixing, and forgetting certain elements in their encounter with other cultures. But how fast can these processes happen? Furthermore, what distinguishes designed transformations of the symbolic order from state-initiated social engineering? Judith Butler was startled by the fact that in 2006 "immigrants were required to take an examination that included the mandatory viewing of images of two gay men kissing to test their 'tolerance' and, hence, capacity to assimilate to Dutch liberalism" (Butler, 2009: 130). It is worth noting that a journalist at Jyllands-Posten named the cartoons as "democratic electroshock therapy" (Klausen, 2009: 20). A "Good Muslim" then is the one who is desensitized. Good, moderate Muslims no longer react to cartoons because they can recognize humor, the playfulness of symbols.

Compromise?

But is this attempt at mediation unreasonable? In the debates on civic nationalism and multiculturalism, the notion of "reasonable accommodation" is predicated on construction of a shared cultural horizon through compromise on the side of both the minority and the majority (Taylor & Bouchard, 2007). So far, I have discussed how the minority was subjected to certain compromises. Let us look at the other side of the debate as well.

There was some discontent during public meetings between Superkilen's designers and ethnic Danes, as the white community preferred a conventional park with green spaces and promenades (Steiner, 2014: 25). As Akšamija's report shows, some residents "were irritated by the choice of the red and black colours for the park, as they were imagining a more traditional park design" (15). Contrary to their desire, they were given an asphalted space with a boxing ring, a bus station sign in Arabic, and giant array loudspeakers, which the designers had intentionally included as a subversive response to complaints about loud music. One could ask why taxpayers' money was spent on a project that does not seem to serve white Danes? These "compromises" are not on the same level, but the fact that a park was conceived as an experimental site for negotiation of identities is indeed remarkable. Furthermore, the majority of signs and urban furniture was not subjected to remix. The Moroccan fountain, for example, remains as "original" as it possibly could. In the case of the object I examined (crescent-tooth), the designers made no changes to what they saw in the photo.

But what if the designers had used the "original" crescent and star instead of this simulacrum? Would it have meant that Muslim minorities and their culture are accepted as they are without any need to change, that is, without cultural assimilation? Islamophobic voices might have argued that unmediated representations of Islamic symbolism herald the triumph of Islamism, because the domination of religious signs over public space goes against secular neutrality. Drawing on the same logic, one can also suggest that granting overt representations will embolden Islamists for more consequential demands such as inclusions of space for daily prayers in public schools and universities.

But, if non-white immigrants with radically diverse backgrounds are arbitrarily identified as Muslims, why should not their representations reflect that "Muslimness?" Ironically, when it comes to immigration and border policies or surveillance and policing, refugees and immigrants are flagged as (potentially dangerous) Muslims, but with regards to representations, they deemed cool and welcoming of compromise.

The Neighborhood: from Political Economy to Cultural Politics

The Nørrebro district has long been a troubled precinct, with its "problems" shifting from strikes to anti-establishment demonstrations to urban riots. Census data from the 1880s show that the area was home to guest workers from other parts of Denmark as well as other countries within Europe (Nielsen, 2012). This was the time when labor movements could organize their resistance against exploitations through unions. On May 5, 1872, thousands of workers protested the "long working hours," and the Battle of Commons became the hallmark of anti-establishment resistance and "struggle for recognition" (Schmidt, 2012: 98). Social tensions were carried through even during the Nazi occupation. In summer 1944, protesters set a department store on fire because the owner was known for being a Nazi sympathizer. In the next couple of decades after the war, however, the demography of the district begun to change. Similar to many industrial centers in Europe in the 1960s, Nørrebro "became a locus for a significant guest worker immigration from countries such as Pakistan and Morocco" (Schmidt, 2012: 98-99).

Despite the influx of non-white immigrants, the political space was able to absorb the "problem" of immigration. Until the 70s, migrant workers—some from the former colonies—were not seen as social or economic threats. They were living in working-class housing blocks in industrial cities along with other workers, some from neighboring European countries. Although the States had no strategy for integration, the workplace and its culture helped immigrants to become part of the larger working-class population. Socialist and communist unions also offered a space for solidarity around shared struggles. Cultural integration was not much of a challenge either. Factories and building sites helped to instill a culture of work, which through its porosity and elasticity, would facilitate integration.

As industries left metropolitan areas in the 80s, urban centers began to lose their economic vitality. In this period, many European city districts suffered from long-term financial crises. Copenhagen was at the brink of bankruptcy. The struggling central city was characterized by a series of interconnected malaise: "de-industrialization, suburbanization, high unemployment rates, high welfare costs, an outdated housing market and strong ethnic and income segregation" (Larsen & Möller, 2013: 2). Unemployment was followed by crimes, delinquency, and marginality.

Nørrebro has been at the center of the national debate on immigration. "Throughout the 1970s and 1980s," Jørgen Nielsen (2012) argues, "squatters and later on radical leftist activists used Nørrebro streets for protest" (Schmidt, 2012, 96). In 1982, to appease social unrest, "the municipality granted a group of youth the rights to use the former Folkets Hus (the People's House)" (Schmidt, 99). The House soon became the epicenter of anti-establishment activities. With the shift to neoliberal politics of privatization in the '80s, not only did the discourse surrounding migrant workers lose its positive overtone, but this era was coincident with the rise of anti-immigrant sentiments. In 2003, Pia Kjærsgaard, the leader of the right-wing populist Danish People's Party (Dansk Folkeparti), expresses her longing for a peaceful past. In setting the stage for the urgency of action, her article, "Give Us Back Nørrebro," postulated: "this country will work on getting back Nørrebro, so that tolerance and liberalism can once again make its way north of Queen Louise's Bridge" (Kärrholm, 2015: 119).

The language of anti-immigrant nationalism marks a radical drift in the perceptions of the area from the mid-nineties. If the slogan for the political left was "[L]et's help people even if they're Muslims or immigrants," today, the discourse of the center-left and Social Democrats has leaned toward populist rhetoric: "We have to take care of Danish people first" (Richard, 2018).

Despite Copenhagen's revitalized economy, the national unemployment rate had cast its shadow on the city. The transformation of the metropolis "from a working-class city [...] to a middle-class city" can be traced in spatial terms, where the gentrification of poor neighborhoods has created areas with a high concentration of "trash proletariat" (Larsen & Möller, 2013: 6). Larsen and Möller note that spatial segregation is targeted at poor "ethnic Danes" as well as "the immigrants and their descendants" (5). Contrasting identities of "the extremes of high society and dark ghetto" are not merely class-based; the divide also is registered across ethnic lines.

In 2008, "one of the worst riots in Denmark" broke out. This was not a leftist outcry, nor a right-wing march against the immigrants. This time, ethnic minorities, especially young Muslim men who were frustrated by police brutality and other racial discriminations, were at the center of the "anarchy" (Larsen & Möller, 2013: 7). This series of events culminated in the demolition of the notorious Ungdomshuset, the former Folket Hus. Even this radical move—demolishing the locus of resistance—did not exterminate the root of the problem. Moreover, economic and social problems have now found an explicitly spatial dimension.

Critics who examined the Superkilen project were aware of this context. Luis Fernández-Galiano, a member of the 2016 Master Jury of the Aga Khan Award, writes: "Not immune to the deep xenophobic, anti-immigration currents that are slowly eroding the foundations of the European Union, Denmark too is now sadly tarnished by Islamophobia—brought violently to the surface here with the anti-mosque campaigns of the Danish People's Party" (Mostafavi, 2016: 27). Denmark is not alone in hostility against Muslim immigrants. The infamous debates on minarets in Switzerland are symptomatic of the same tension, namely, can "Muslims" have cultural representations within cityscapes? For centuries, European societies were relatively homogeneous in terms of their ethnic and cultural outlooks—argues Diana L. Eck (2006). Migrations and exchanges have always existed, but due to the slow rate of change, gradual transformations were not perceived as threats. Today, on the contrary, "formerly homogenous European societies" that for centuries had imagined their communities "along more unitary lines" find themselves challenged by the emergence of multicultural and multiethnic social formations.

Failed Integration and Stigmatized Spaces

National security experts are quick to diagnose a common malaise in ethnic and low-income neighborhoods in Europe. Community withdrawal, or *"repli communautaire,"* refers to the social conditions in which certain communities, particularly non-white immigrants who live in public housing complexes, close themselves off from the rest of society (Lapeyronnie & Courtois, 2008). As politics creates more borders for and around precarious immigrants, the immigrants, too, cocoon themselves in identarian closures. Communitarianism in turn contributes to the ghettoization of immigrant living spaces. The danger is that these zones become a fertile ground for fundamentalist ideologies and eventually radicalization.

These spaces are characterized by the following traits: 1) low-income housing with high rates of unemployment or precarious employment; 2) dilapidated housing environment; 3) poor public services; 4) high rates of school dropouts, and above all, 5) high concentration of ethno-racial minorities (Bancel & Blanchard & Ahmed Boubeker, 2015).

As I mentioned earlier, Nørrebro is on Denmark's ghetto list and is subjected to "anti-ghetto laws" (Barry & Sorensen, 2018). Similar to other European countries, Denmark identifies ghettos through the following criteria: "unemployment rates over 20%, 50% of its population from non-Western countries or are descendants of migrants from non-Western countries, relatively low-income, low education level, and the presence of criminal activity" (Turan, 2021: 62).

Two types of questions emerge. First, why did immigrants from the Middle East or North Africa concentrate in these neighborhoods in the first place, and why they not able to find alternative housing? The discourse surrounding communitarianism is predicated on the assumption that immigrants prefer to stick together, which is to say, to self-segregate. Second, how have non-white urban outcasts been identified by their assumed religion and religiosity, and why is culture blamed for communitarianism?

Unlike what has been propagated by the popular media about Muslim's unwillingness to "integrate into the wider society," the majority of Muslims have a strong desire to integrate, and almost half of the Muslim population wants to be seen as Danish (Larsen & Möller, 2013: 20). Yet only around ten percent of "Muslims" in Denmark "believe that others see them as Danish." While the multiculturalist conception of "Danishness" is predicated on "ethnic, cultural, and religious diversity," the growing anti-immigrant sentiments in the West— along with malevolent claims about "Muslim invasion," or "reverse colonialization"—has challenged the limits of Danish multiculturalism (Schmidt, 2012: 96). To represent Muslims as a minority group that can never be included into Danishness, there is a need to resuscitate what has been long fought against: Europe's Christian identity. Anxious about their ethno-cultural identity, conservative Danes have realized that being Dane and Christian are inextricably bound. This view is integral to "traditional Danish culture" to such a degree which leaves little room for cultural differences: "any model of multiculturalism which suggest the presence of parallel communities," may be construed as "a threat to national unity and social cohesion" (Schmidt, 2012: 232).

Today, the return to civilizational discourse is a way of alienating non-white immigrants and citizens. This operates on two levels. The emphasis on Judeo-Christian civilization, a term that for historians of religion is rather an oxymoron, is a polemic that frames Islam as an incompatible ideology. Couched in civilizational discourse, there lurks also the spectre of racism that insists that Europe was, and indeed should remain, a white, Christian civilization.

While many immigrants aspire to "[be] Muslim and Danish at the same time," some prefer "to avoid cultural assimilation." (Schmidt, 2012: 232). Why? Under real or imagined discrimination and in response to racist treatments, minorities feel that any form of assimilation may cause them to lose "their collective cultural and religious identity." Against this anxiety, they enter in an obsessional relationship with particular elements of their culture. This is what Charles Taylor (1994) calls the politics of "cultural survival." Since many constitutive elements of their cultures cannot be sustained outside the "original" social milieu—think of holidays that are calendar-specific and that only make sense when accompanied with food, music, and celebrations—it is again religion that represents itself as the last bastion of identity. The more these minorities feel threatened, that is, the more the external grip tightens on their "ways of life," the more they tend to essentialize their religion. To protect their identity, it is not their culture that is emphasized, but the most stereotypical elements of religion.

Despite the variegated cultural and ethnic backgrounds of the immigrant inhabitants of Nørrebro, they were perceived as a homogeneous population. A socio-spatial study acknowledged that, contrary to the dominant political discourse, the Muslim community was not a singular entity with rigid boundaries (At Home in Europe Project, 2011). The report also suggested that individuals with a certain "cultural and ethnic background" would be automatically perceived as Muslim "even though they may be atheists or followers of other religions" (23). Not only does this blanket identification serve the conservative political agenda to blame religion for their economic precarity, but this false flag also attracts radical Islamic groups who wish to turn these segregated spaces into havens for radicalization. The more the State stigmatize these neighborhoods, the more chance would emerge for them to be turned into what Olivier Roy calls "Islamized spaces" (1994).

The question that I am concerned with here is not whether Muslims are racialized, but how racialization works. It happens at the crossroads of categories that have nothing to do with the color of skin: clothing and surfaces attached to the body (headscarves), architecture and surfaces that serve as the background for the body (stigmatized neighborhoods), images that exert their forces on the body (media representations), names that foreground the body (non-Western names), etc. It does not come as a surprise that some change their Muslim/Arab names "to increase their chance of employment" (Abid Ullah Jan, 2006, 180).

Architecture is not a neutral vessel that contains or represents social relations; it constructs its own subjects. A stigmatized public housing project is not simply a space inhabited by the urban underclass. Since the dilapidated place is associated with migrant workers who are experiencing unemployment, anyone who comes to inhabit that space is seen through a lens that colors their identity with particular racial, class, and cultural (if not religious) tones. Incidentally, an undesirable neighborhood with crumbling public housing complexes is the only housing option that unemployed immigrants can afford. The State also accommodates refugees and the displaced population in such complexes.

By the "virtue" of living in these already-segregated and stigmatized spaces, the subjects are automatically perceived as urban outcasts with a set of cultural associations.

Superkilen as Extension of the Institution of the Border

While the concept of national border marks the territorial boundary, the actual extent of its symbolic, legal, and material presence is not confined to the ultimate line that separates geopolitical entities. Even at the edges of the territory, borders are operative not merely upon their material force and physical impermeability, but by the political and symbolic power that support them. This is to say that borders are always already institutional. Their function is sustained upon forces, real and imagined, that themselves are buttressed by legal and penal infrastructures as well as police and military entities. I use the *institution of the border* to refer to physical, symbolic, and legal apparatuses that control the processes of inclusion and exclusion. By determining who is permitted to traverse frontiers, the institution of the border creates not only an Schmittian binary between those who (fully) belong and those who don't, but it also establishes hierarchies between the population based on their relationship to the function of this very institution. Indispensable to biopolitics and key to political economy of nation, the institution of the border expands its presence inward as much as it spreads outward. Étienne Balibar (2001) captures this process of "thickening" of borders succinctly:

> The borders of new politico-economic entities, the function of which is to preserve the sovereignty of the State, are no longer situated at the edge of the territories. They are scattered almost everywhere, where they effectuate and control the movement of information, people, and things. (1)

This thickening encompasses physical apparatuses of control at all scales—from fortified and militarized zones at national borders to ever-expanding refugee camps that are meant to protect larger political entities. It does not come as a surprise that although Turkey has never been recognized as part of Europe (not EU nor Eurozone), it is, nonetheless, a NATO member. Turkey has thus become the border for Europe, a scaled-up border checkpoint that protects Europe from Syrian refugees and the like. While externally the institution of the border exceeds the limits of Europe itself, internally, it penetrates the domestic realm through surveillance, profiling, and policing.

Charged with anxieties of the Other, the institution of the border cuts through the entire social field. When the society is stratified by different types of borders—citizenship, class, race, gender, religion—*bordering* becomes the social practice par excellence. Architecture is no stranger here. Urban politics mirrors the exclusionary practices that are operative in border politics. As an "ideological state apparatus," to use Althusser's formula, such projects are designed to not only keep certain categories of immigrants outside, but also to sideline subaltern citizens. "Outside" in this scheme is not confined to territoriality. By being confined to stigmatized places and the living conditions that do not afford certain types of freedom, marginalized population are being kept outside the sphere of politics in a Habermasian sense.

Seen in this light, Superkilen is an extension of the institution of the border that has reached the heart of urban life. It is a community-scale testing ground for biopolitics. Why should cultural representation of non-white immigrants have something to do with Islam? The fact that the designers assumed that non-white citizens living in the area need cultural elements from elsewhere (their "original" homeland) begs the question whether they will ever "pass the border" and be accepted as fellow Danes?

Let us now see the park in a positive light. Superkilen borders between the interiority of the domestic realm and the exteriority of the public space. Positioned between the two, the park brings them into "play" to create the "third space" of translation and negotiation. The point of the participatory design was to turn the inbetween space into a quasi-private zone for the neighborhood, an outdoor "living room" or a shared "backyard" for otherwise isolated communities. Superkilen provides a chance for isolated communities to feel that they have a space that belongs to them, precisely because they have helped to create it. At the same time, it becomes a quasi-public zone when it juxtaposes different cultural symbols within a universal space of representations. It mediates between particular cultures and the mainstream, giving the former the means to become part of the geoculture of modernity, to use Wallerstein's (1991) terminology. The fact that different communities now use the park for organizing different events is indicative of its success in building bridges. "Superkilen now provides a meeting point for people in the community," writes Akšamija. "The site," she continues, "is now associated with vivid activity" (2016, 28).

Moreover, if the institution of the border is concerned with drawing lines between inside and outside, between us and them, the Superkilen park—which provides a site for grafting identities by blurring the lines between them—poses a serious challenge to this institution. Finally, one might regard the botched attempt at recognition of immigrant communities as a part of the diversity of city life. No matter how ambivalent the "participatory" process of Superkilen was, the city of Copenhagen is a desirable political form because it strives to be open and inclusive. Interestingly, Iris Young's (2011) defense of the normative function of cities is fitting here, as one can see Superkilen as "heterogeneous, plural, and playful, a place where people witness and appreciate diverse cultural expressions that they do not share and do not fully understand" (241).

If the neoliberal State with its privatizing agenda is not genuinely invested in helping immigrants to integrate through market economy, then assimilation through spatial means represents itself as a viable solution. The designers of Superkilen were not naïve to assume that the park will function as an ultimate solution and dissolve social tensions. Rather, they conceived the park, I think, as an open layout, a third space, for construction of hybrid identities and cultural fusions.

At a time when multicultural politics in Europe has reached a point of impasse, Superkilen seems to offer an alternative. The problem with differentialist multiculturalism is that it accepts cultures as given. Two vices ensue. First, this uncritical acceptance ends up foreclosing particular cultures into reified entities with fixed essences. Second, it also indulges the desire of different cultural communities for self-perpetuation. This type of multiculturalism can breed phenomena such as culturalism, identitarianism, and communitarianism. While multiculturalism seems to carry stigma, other vocabularies are taking its place. Interculturalism, for example, rejects the multi-cultural fragmentation of the society. (Bouchard, 2011: 468) It has become clear that keeping immigrants excluded in spatial and cultural closures inevitably yields greater problems.

Conclusion: The Question of Political Inclusivity

The park mediates between public space and private domain of social isolation. It creates an intermediary zone for negotiation of differences. Superkilen offers cultural representations, recognizing and affirming particular identities, while also helping to transform those very identities into more open, hybrid, and inbetween subjective constellations. Why should I be critical of this twofold aim?

The design creates a lively and exciting public space, but it does little in creating an inclusive public sphere—understood as "an arena of political deliberation and participation" (Harvey, 2006: 20). Superkilen succeeds in introducing a democratic regime of representations, but the question remains if political inclusivity can be limited to representations. As Iris Young notes, "[d]emocratization requires the development of grass-roots institutions of local discussion and decision making. Such democratization is meaningless unless the decisions include participation in economic power" (Young, 249). I am not merely critical of the design because it did not adequately include immigrants in decisions about design. Neither is my dismay due to the fact that in deciding on the nature of representation, the designers "did not let neighborhood dwellers exert any influence over decisions," or that the people of the area "had less than a 10% input on overall decision making." (Turan, 2021) The problem rather is that the design depoliticized what was at its core a political question: how to create an egalitarian public sphere beyond representations? It seems that, in spite of the façade of democratic inclusivity, cultural representation and political empowerment were kept separate. As Mark Lilla (2018) would have framed it, the project is rather an "empty gestures of recognition and 'celebration'" (14), because it absolves the State from taking meaningful measures in helping immigrants to integrate.

The politics of the neoliberal State blames its social malaise as well as its economic shortcomings on its immigrant population. To absolve itself from the responsibility of providing sustainable employment and public infrastructure while also masking its racial biases, the State blames immigrants for not having the desire to fit into the mold of entrepreneurial success. Since race/ethnicity-based discrimination falls outside the limits of political-correctness, something else should be blamed as the obstacle to participation in public life. It is not, then, unemployment and discrimination that marginalize immigrants; it is their religion that does not allow integration.

They can never become good citizens, because their religion is incompatible with modernity and liberalism, or so we are told.

We are dealing with the aestheticization of the politics of integration. Spatial identity politics does more than re-presenting ethnic communities. Through participation, certain voices are heard and turned into images. This is important because an inclusive representation is crucial for equitable distribution of resources. Yet this very process of translating voices is never neutral. What about voices that could not have been translated into "cool" images, those that were cacophonous—demanding more equitable rights, social services, and sustainable jobs? The constituency seems to have been given agency, but it was a prescribed agency. Incidentally, a grassroots initiative that tried to formulate the needs of the residents was sidelined (Bloom, 2020). Architecture that is limited to curated representations conceals social antagonisms and relations of domination more that it reveals them. Important to note that Nørrebro is subject to anti-ghetto laws which aim to displace those living in low-income houses by either demolition or privatization (Danish Transport, Construction and Housing Authority, 2019). As Mohsen Mostafavi has noted, the "success" of Superkilen has contributed to the gentrification of the area. Who is Superkilen serving? As the cost of housing increases, the urban poor will be further pushed to the margins. The "right to the city," Richard Sennett argues, is increasingly "a bourgeois prerogative" (Harvey, 2006: 20). At the end, the process only reinforces the domination of the rich, ethnic Danes over political space.

Design projects are meant to be solutions to given problems. The Municipality of Copenhagen misrecognized the problem of urban marginality and economic precarity as cultural. The reference to the cartoons controversy distracts attention from larger social discontents and structural issues. Following this misdiagnosis, the solution was also conceived as cultural, namely, giving more representations. Furthermore, the project "celebrates" cultural difference. Yet, the more it emphasizes the notion of difference, the more it frames immigrants as outsiders. Why did the designers assume that the culture of ethnic citizens is different from the mainstream (white) culture? Still, upon what measures did the designers assume that non-white inhabitants of the neighborhood were immigrants and not citizens? To bring objects from other places (including Muslim countries) reinforces the idea that non-white citizens are not accepted as citizens.

It is worth remembering that the district was once the center of political resistance. The State's ultimate solution was the demolition of the "House of People." The House was doomed because it was a place for the opposition to organize and turn their resistance to a more effective force in demanding political rights. What would it have meant for Superkilen to include a community center? Would it turn into another "House of People," or a union of sorts where unemployed immigrants could organize and formulate their political demands, such as non-precarious jobs and more social services? Against this image, designing a park that aims at building inclusivity through representations seems insufficient, if not irrelevant, to the question of political inclusivity.[4]

References

Aga Kahn Development Network (AKDN) (2016). Superkilen [Online]. Available at: http://akdn.org/architecture/ project/Superkilen (Accessed 9 May 2017).

Akšamija, A (2016). "Azra Akšamija | Superkilen On-site Review Report." Archnet (Aga Khan Award for Architecture and Aga Khan Historical Cities Program, Retrieved April 26, 2022, from Archnet: https://www.archnet.org/ publications/10687

Aga Khan Award for Architecture winners announced | Aga Khan Documentation Center. (n.d.). Retrieved April 25, 2022, from https://libraries.mit.edu/akdc/2016/ 10/06/aga-khan-award-for-architecture-winners-announced/

Asad, T., Brown, W., Butler, J., Mahmood, S., & UPSO (2013). Is critique secular?: Blasphemy, injury, and free speech. Fordham University Press.

Balibar, Étienne. (2004). We, the people of Europe?: Reflections on transnational citizenship. Princeton University Press.

Bloom, B. A. (2013). Superkilen: Participatory Park Extreme! Kritik.

Bouchard, G. (2011). What is Interculturalism? MacGill Law Journal McGill Law Journal, 56(2), 435–468.

Butler, J. (2013). The Sensibility of Critique: Response to Asad and Mahmood. 95–128.

CANactions School. (2017, June 14). Personal Public Space – Martin Rein-Cano / CANactions Festival 2017. https://www.youtube.com/watch?v=0MnMt_xmaLA

Eck, D. L. (2007). Prospects for Pluralism: Voice and Vision in the Study of Religion. Journal of the American Academy of Religion, 75(4), 743–776. https://doi.org/10.1093/ jaarel/lfm061

Barry, E., & Selsoe, S. M., (2018). In Denmark, Harsh New Laws for Immigrant 'Ghettos'—The New York Times. Retrieved April 25, 2022, from https://www.nytimes.com/2018/07/01/world/europe/denmark-immigrant-ghettos.html

For 40 år siden kørte sidste sporvogn i Danmark [40 years ago the last tram in Denmark departed]. (2012). http://www.letbaner.dk/nyheder/00423/

Fraser, N., & Honneth, A. (2003). Redistribution or recognition?: A political-philosophical exchange. Verso.

Gauchet, M. (2015). La religion dans la démocratie: Parcours de la laïcité.

[4] This essay benefited from the insightful readership of Carl Ernst, Michele Lamprakos, Burak Erdim, Sandy Marshall, Shayna Mehas, Nathan Jumper, Alexandra Masgras, Daniel Jost, Emily Shuman, Elsa Costa, Elliot Mamet, Iris Gilad, Qiu Lin, and Alberto La Rosa Rojas.

Ghettolisten—Definition af en ghetto. (n.d.). Regeringen.dk. Retrieved April 27, 2022, from https://www.regeringen.dk/nyheder/2017/ghetto-listen-2017-to-nye-omraader-tilfoejet-fem- fjernet/ghettolisten-definition-af-en-ghetto/

Harvey, D. (2005). The Political Economy of Public Space. In The Politics of Public Space. Routledge.

Jan A. U. (2006). After Fascism: Muslims and the Struggle for Self-Determination. Pragmatic Pub. Ottawa, ON.

Klausen, J. (2009). The Danish cartoons and modern iconoclasm in the cosmopolitan Muslim diaspora. In Harvard Middle Eastern and Islamic Review, 8 (2009), 86–118.

Klausen, J. (2009). The Cartoons That Shook the World. Yale University Press.

Kärrholm, M. (2015). Urban squares: spatio-temporal studies of design and everyday life in the öresund region. Nordic Academic Press.

Korzybski, A. (2005). Science and sanity: An introduction to non-Aristotelian systems and general semantics. Institute of General Semantics.

Lapeyronnie, D., & Courtois, L. (2008). Ghetto urbain: Ségrégation, violence, pauvreté en France aujourd'hui. Laffont.

Larsen, J. E., & Møller, I. H. (2013). The increasing socioeconomic and spatial segregation and polarization of living conditions in the Copenhagen metropolitan area. 35.

Lawrence, B. B. (1989). Defenders of God: The Fundamentalist Revolt Against the Modern Age. Harper & Row.

Lilla, M. (2018). The Once and Future Liberal: After Identity Politics. Oxford University Press.

Low, S. M., & Smith, N. (2006). The Politics of Public Space. Routledge.

Møller, I. H., & Larsen, J. E. (2015). The Socioeconomic and Ethnic Segregation of Living Conditions in Copenhagen. Revista Crítica de Ciências Sociais, 108, 7–30. https://doi.org/10.4000/rccs.6071

Ozouf, M. (1982). L'École, l'Église et la République, 1871-1914. Éditions Cana/Jean Offredo.

Pitkin, H. F. (1967). The Concept of Representation. University of California Press.

Promulgation de la loi relative à la séparation des Églises et de l'État. (n.d.). Gouvernement.fr. Retrieved April 25, 2022, from https://www.gouvernement.fr/partage/8764-le-9-decembre-1905-est-promulguee-la-loi-%20relative-%C3%A0-la-s%C3%A9paration-des-%C3%89glises-et-de-l-%C3%89tat

Roy, O. (1994). The Failure of Political Islam. Harvard University Press.

Roy, O. (2020). Is Europe Christian? Oxford University Press.

Scott, J. W. (2010). The Politics of the Veil. Princeton University Press.

Steiner, B. (2014). Superkilen: A project by Big, Topotek 1, Superflex. Arvinius & Orfeus.

Superkilen – Superflex. Retrieved April 27, 2022, from https://www.superflex.net/works/superkilen

Superkilen | Aga Khan Development Network. (n.d.). Retrieved April 25, 2022, from https://www.akdn.org/ architecture/project/superkilen

Todd, E. (2015). Qui est Charlie?: Sociologie d'une crise religieuse. Éditions du Seuil.

Turan, B. Y. (2021). Superkilen: Coloniality, citizenship, and border politics. In Landscape Citizenships. (56-78). Routledge.

Venturi R. Scott Brown D. & Izenour S. (1972). Learning from las vegas. MIT Press.

Vivre ensemble: Des projets qui favorisent l'intégration dans 11 villes de l'Union Européenne. (2011). Budapest.

Wallerstein I. M. (1991). Geopolitics and geoculture: essays on the changing world-system. Cambridge University Press; Editions de la Maison des Sciences de l'Homme.

Waterman, T., Wolff, J., & Wall, E. (Eds.). (2021). Landscape Citizenships (1st ed.).

Routledge.

Young, I. M., & Allen, D. S. (2011). Justice and the politics of difference. Princeton University Press.

THE ROLE OF INFORMATIONAL ASYMMETRY IN INTERFAITH COMMUNICATION DURING CONFLICT: A GAME THEORETICAL APPROACH

Serdar Ş. Güner[1] and Nukhet A. Sandal[2]

Introduction

Interfaith communication can be defined as the interactions between religious or political actors belonging to different traditions who communicate with interlocutors on a particular issue, recognizing the importance of the religious dimension in their interactions. Such communication can alter the opinions of the "other" and allow mutual understanding and respect to develop between parties (Laustsen & Waever, 2000). Parties to these sensitive interactions usually find that their decisions depend on the interlocutor's past, the expectations of the interlocutor's future behavior, and trust levels. In this article, we investigate the role of uncertainty about others' sincerity and trustworthiness in interfaith communication, especially in times of political conflict. We draw attention to the tensions between representing a community and reaching out to "the other side." We offer a game-theoretical model of asymmetric information where players are unequal in terms of the information they have vis-à-vis each other's preferences over the possible outcomes of their interaction.

Scholars from various disciplines have written on the basic conditions for successful interfaith communication. Just to give some examples, King (2011:106) lists seven types of interreligious dialogue ranging from "official/institutional dialogue between or among elites chosen by their religions as official representatives" to "spiritual dialogue, in which one learns and engages in the spiritual practices of another religion." Lederach (1995) and Gopin (2002) analyze interreligious communication within the

[1] Serdar Ş. Güner, Associate Professor of International Relations, Bilkent University, Turkey. E-mail: sguner@bilkent.edu.tr.

[2] Nukhet A. Sandal (corresponding author), Associate Professor of Political Science, Ohio University, United States. E-mail: sandal@ohio.edu.

Authors have equally contributed to the manuscript and their names are listed in alphabetical order by surname.

Acknowledgement: This is a reprint of the article which appeared originally in International Journal of Religion: Sheikholharam, E. (2022). The Role of Informational Asymmetry in Interfaith Communication During Conflict: A Game Theoretical Approach, International Journal of Religion, Vol.3, No.1, pp.19-36. DOI: https://doi.org/10.33182/ijor.v3i1.1585. Grateful for the permission granted by IJOR.

context of religious peacebuilding. Focusing on the case of Sierra Leone, Day (2021) argues that interfaith initiatives are more successful when they build on shared cultural ties. Fletcher (2007) investigates interfaith dialogues from theological perspectives. Bender and Cadge (2006), Twiss (2018), and Riitaoja and Dervin (2014) have written at the intersection of the fields of sociology of religion, ethics, and education, respectively. There are also works that address the question of the ideal conditions for interfaith dialogue. Cornille (2013:30), for example, counts humility, commitment, interconnection and hospitality as epistemological requirements for interreligious dialogue. Cilliers (2002) states that justice, reconciliation, forgiveness and truth are the pillars of interfaith dialogue. Orton (2016) poses seven key questions for theory, policy and practice in interfaith dialogue, including "Who is involved?" "Who is missing?" and "What is the dialogue for?"

Overall, the literature on interfaith dialogue and its success rarely discusses the implications of the rationality assumption for interreligious interactions. One reason for this gap might be the belief that rational choice and optimization models are not deemed suitable for studying religion and religious behavior. Contrary to this belief, there are rational choice analyses of religion and secularization in the field. Habel and Grant (2013) use formal theory and simulations to explore "whether demand for religion and government increase in response to security risk". Young (1997) has investigated how the rationality assumption is used and criticized in studies of religion. Iannaccone (1995: 79–81) has argued that the rational choice method has the virtue of unifying alternative intuitions and explanations. Excluding the rationality assumption prevents researchers from obtaining counterintuitive and engaging results. Iannaccone (1994:1205–1209) has also offered game-theoretical models to explain the competition among churches to expand their membership and demonstrates that the demands for strict loyalty and a rigid adherence to lifestyles these churches impose on their disciples solve problems of free-riding connected with benefiting from religious activities without paying the price. Similar to Iannaccone, in the field of evolutionary religious studies, Sosis and Alcorta (2003) find that costly signals of commitment solve the free-rider problem.

Such rational choice analyses of religion have not, for the most part, explored interfaith initiatives. Those that attempt to use a game theoretical approach to study these initiatives remain rather descriptive. One such example is Malik's (2013) use of game theory metaphors to study the roots of "A Common Word Between Us," an open letter from Muslim scholars to Christian leaders. The work that comes closest to our topic of interest is by Vüllers, who argues that "religious actors do interest-based calculations before working for peace" (2019:5) and finds that "representatives of a religious group will engage in formal peace activism if the costs are modest and their identity is threatened by a civil war" (2019: 16). The calculations Vüllers refers to would become a little more complicated under informational asymmetries in a game setting.

In an attempt to complement the works mentioned above, we aim to contribute to the interfaith communications literature by proposing a game model to advance alternative interpretations of interreligious communication cast as a strategic interaction. Our approach opens the door for modeling different priorities of the actors and contexts under which interfaith interactions happen. Not every actor engages in interfaith communication with pure communicative motives. Sometimes, these dialogues are expected to serve political ends and are used to signal commitment to one's values, rather than reaching an agreement. The same reasoning and modeling can be applied to religious violence, competition among religious organizations, and the policymaking of religious actors including individuals, political parties, and states.

The game-theoretical model accentuates the strategic uncertainty dialogue participants face. As players, they must think about how others would respond when they cooperate and defect; their decisions depend on their expectations of how others will behave. A participant is less likely to engage in cooperation if this contradicts norms of the group, sect, or political party they belong to. If everyone else cooperates, some participants might actually prefer defection, being afraid of peer pressure or wanting to establish a reputation of commitment to their values and not giving in. They might think that if they cooperated and did not challenge the other actor, they would be targets of home-side criticism and face social exclusion. Thus, some interlocutors might prefer to be aligned with exclusive group norms in a dialogue, hurting the possibility of cooperative exchanges with the other. The game identifies strategic conditions that neutralize and outweigh such preferences that are not in the spirit of open and cooperative communications.

The game theoretical approach to interfaith communications—especially in the context of conflicts—assumes only a weak form of rationality; players' preferences over outcomes are consistent and transitive. Thus, here *rationality means consistency*—players have transitive preferences over the outcomes of the interactions and objectives they try to realize by joining interfaith dialogues. Instead of having an objective utility function quantifying agents' preferences and agents' choices of maximizing utility, the key is the consistency of choices as depending on consistent preference orderings. O'Neill (2001: 289) states that:

> Rational choice theory refers to the general approach that parties pursue their material self-interest, pay attention to objective likelihoods and maximize their expectations in a conscious, calculated way. In fact, game-theoretical models do not necessarily belong to rational choice theory [...] the only vestige of 'rationality' required now is that players judge likelihoods and pursue goals, and this is a weak connection. Players' goals may be far from self-interest, and their probabilities may be quite unreasonable. [...] People's beliefs must be consistent; their actions must be consistent; and the two in combination must be consistent.

Under the assumption of consistency, the models can be usefully applied in research if they generate informative suggestions and interpretations vis-à-vis interfaith communications considered as strategic interactions.

Against this background, we do not argue that games perfectly correspond to reality. From the scientific realist angle, interfaith dialogues as described and observed constitute the reality; nothing else counts much (Devitt, 1997). We are after interpretations of reality, not explanations. Our view is centrally instrumentalist, and it represents an alternative to the scientific realist approach of providing objective explanations (Friedman, 1953). In other words, our game model is highly idealized. The game rules about players and their preferences, sequences of moves, and information conditions can be considered much like physicists' frictionless planes and surfaces (Cartwright, 2010). Like many game theorists, we assume preferences without exploring their cultural and personal origins—no such goal is feasible in an article-length study. The main feature of the game is simply rigor. The model aims to generate interpretations and further questions with the goal of better understanding interfaith communication, especially considering the different possible motives of the actors.

We deduce equilibria from assumed rules, implying the most logical responses of players in their interaction. Hence, one must read the equilibria and their interpretations of games as consequences limited by the requirements of the mathematical tractability and a condition of weak rationality. The perfect Bayesian equilibria of the games represent how agents make choices based on their preferences under conditions of limited information. Limited or asymmetric information refers to an interlocutor's uncertainty about the other's sincerity in conducting a dialogue —namely, the other's preference orderings over the outcomes of the interaction.

Information Asymmetry in Interreligious Interactions During Conflict

In strategic interactions, including interfaith ones, interlocutors calculate how much they will concede partly based on their perception of how sincere and committed their counterparts are. Participants usually prioritize survival of their own religious and cultural system (Geertz, 1973). Hence, interfaith dialogues can be troubling for some actors who might think that such interactions will compromise their religious views and social standing. A group member's participation in an interfaith interaction may thus be seen as a breach within a community of the common understanding of "the other" and legitimacy of the other's views (Scott, 2000: 823).

The participants in interfaith interactions indeed operate under different conditions and may have different goals. Ideally, the participants in interfaith dialogue would aim to understand each other, develop relationships of mutual respect and transform their own beliefs in the pursuit of an "ultimate reality" (Neufeldt, 2011: 349). However, some interfaith interactions, which Kolvenbach and Pittau (1999) have called "doctrinal assertive dialogues," might aim at proselytization without the intention of engaging with the other faith on equal footing. The goal of interfaith behavior can also change over time. Takim (2004: 345), for example, draws attention to how increased dialogue and interaction between Muslims and Christians since 9/11 "represents a significant paradigm shift, a shift from attempts at 'conversion of' to […] a 'conversation with' the other."

According to Iannaccone (1995), religious goods satisfy the spiritual needs and demands of religious consumers. In this sense, interfaith dialogues constitute markets of exchange where principles of supply and demand apply. Naturally, these goods mean different things to different agents interacting with each other. For example, Putnam's (1988) two-level games could be applied to religious leaders' efforts to balance the demands of their community and the need to communicate and work with the representatives of other religious groups. For the outsider, it might be challenging to understand the constraints, perspectives and different personalities within a faith group. In this context, our game theoretical model's central motive is to incorporate informational asymmetries in interfaith communications, which existing studies of interreligious communication have so far not done.

Uncertainties and suspicion in interfaith communications become even more prevalent in conflict settings. Not every actor who participates in interfaith communication has pure intentions to reach out and come to a compromise. In her review of religion, peacebuilding and interreligious communication, Kadayifci-Orellana (2013: 162) notes that "during times of conflict, mutual distrust makes any interaction with the 'other' suspicious." Abu Nimer and colleagues (2007: 67) warn that—especially in conflict settings where there is asymmetric power distribution, like in Israel–Palestine—interfaith meetings can be "perceived as another forum serving majority and cultural domination." Political conflicts can hinder trust between religious communities and leaders. Bunza (2016) states that "the complex nature of the country [Nigeria] in terms of ethnic, tribal, and regional composition, coupled with the political and economic rivalry among these regions and tribes" created conditions of mistrust and prevented effective interreligious (Muslim–Christian) initiatives.

Similarly, Perica (2001: 58–61) notes that the suspicion between the Serbian Orthodox Church and the Croatian Catholic Church, coupled with the nationalist ideologies associated with each church, prevented them from forging a long-lasting alliance against their common enemy, communism. There may also be a tension between "the demands of political activism (in which it may be desirable to minimize difference with potential allies) and religious recruitment (which may require the magnification of differences)" (Jelen, 2001:21). This tension has been the concern of religious and political actors, who might consider joining interfaith or ecumenical initiatives, yet end up not doing so due to the fear of negative reaction from their own communities.

Religious communities are socially constructed entities with rules and related practices. In this spirit, religious leaders vary in their boundaries and sensitivities. Haddad and Fischbach (2015: 433), for example, in their study of interfaith dialogue in Lebanon, emphasize that "religious leaders in Lebanon have first and foremost an interest in preserving clear boundaries for their communities." With a desire to protect such boundaries, the participant would be concerned about striking a balance between being involved in a genuine dialogue with representatives of different religions and accountability to fellow followers of the religion. The participant might "pretend" that they are interested in communications with others and then instrumentally use these interfaith interactions to solidify their standing and further their goals in their own religious community. Therefore, in our particular game, we take into account the possibility of both motives—namely, a genuine desire to cooperate with the other toward achieving a goal, or pretending that the participant is interested in communications, only to use the interactions for instrumental motives and rather than a desire to understand and work with the partner. Once again, this is a critical distinction that has not been studied in the relevant literature, and through our modeling, we are working toward filling this gap.

An Interfaith Asymmetric Information Game

Figure 1. The Game Tree

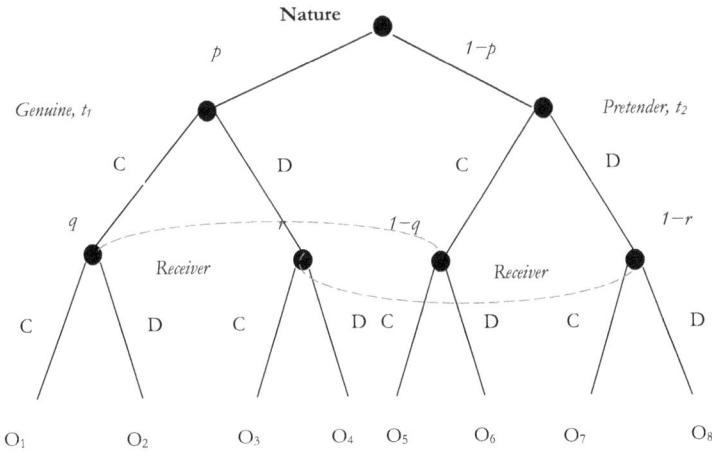

The game stylizes interactions between participants in an instance of interfaith communication. It simplifies the reality of participants who can choose numerous moves by modeling only two players having two actions at their disposal. **The Sender** starts the dialogue by selecting either cooperation or defection. **The Receiver** reacts to the Sender with either defection or cooperation. The sequence of moves leads to four categories of outcomes: 1) the Sender and the Receiver cooperate, generating the outcome of mutual cooperation; 2) the Sender cooperates but the Receiver does not (which indicates the unilateral cooperation and commitment of the Sender); 3) the Sender defects but the Receiver cooperates (which indicates the unilateral cooperation and commitment of the Receiver), and; 4) the Sender and the Receiver defect leading to the outcome of mutual defection. The game ends when each player takes an action, and an outcome is reached.

Informational Asymmetry

The game assumes the existence of two sets of people involved in the dialogue. The first set of actors sincerely care about cooperation and a genuine exchange of views. The second set mostly cares about political gains and establishing a reputation of being inflexible (to reiterate/signal their commitment to their religious/political values). The Receiver and the Genuine Sender (**the Genuine**) come from the first set, as represented in different faith traditions. The Sender with ulterior political motives (**the Pretender**) belongs to the second set.

The game presents an informational asymmetry based on this division. The Receiver observes the Sender's cooperation or defection but is uncertain whether the cooperation or defection reflects the action of the Genuine or Pretender version of the Sender. She knows that the Sender's cooperation does not prove that he is, in fact, genuine. If she reciprocates the Sender's cooperation, she might also reach an understanding with the Pretender, even with the Pretender's ulterior motives. Thus, the Receiver does not know what exact outcome the Sender prefers in the interaction, making her open to the Sender's manipulations. Both the Genuine and the Pretender know the Receiver's preferences over the outcomes of the interaction. The Receiver is well informed that both the Genuine and the Pretender are informed of her preferences and her limited information.

What can the Receiver do to prevent being cheated by the Sender? She can try to decipher the Sender's move to assess whether she is facing the Genuine or the Pretender based on her beliefs about the Sender's preferences. The Receiver is assumed to entertain such beliefs before she observes the Sender's move, yet these beliefs in the form of likelihoods remain unchanged after her observation. If, for example, the Receiver believes that she is facing the Pretender or the Genuine with an 80 percent and a 20 percent chance, respectively, before the Sender moves, then the Receiver will continue to hold the belief that she is interacting with the Pretender or the Genuine with the same respective chances after she observes cooperation or defection by the Sender.

This means that priors are equal to posteriors per game theory jargon. If both types choose C, then the Receiver's information set is reached via two distinct paths. Nature picks the Sender Type 1 with probability p and the Type 1 chooses C by certainty. Hence, we have p as the likelihood of the first path. Similarly, the second path's probability is the multiplication of $1-p$ and the likelihood of the Type 2's choice of C by certainty. The Receiver's belief that she is at the left node of her information set is the ratio $\frac{p.1}{p.1+(1-p).1} = p = q$. The Receiver's belief that she is at the right node of her information set then becomes $1 - q = \frac{(1-p).1}{(1-p).1+(p).1} = 1 - p$.

Strategies

The Sender and the Receiver have four strategies in their mutual communications. The Sender's strategies are as follows: "cooperate regardless of what my preferences are," "cooperate if I am the Genuine, defect if I am the Pretender," "defect if I am the Genuine, cooperate if I am the Pretender," and "defect regardless of what my preferences are— that is, regardless of whether I am the Genuine or the Pretender." The Receiver does not condition her strategies upon her type. The strategies of the Receiver are "cooperate regardless of the Sender's action," "cooperate if the Sender cooperates and defect if the Sender defects," "defect if the Sender cooperates and cooperate if the Sender defects," and "defect regardless of the Sender's action."

The Sender strategies of "cooperate regardless of what my preferences are" and "defect regardless of what my preferences are" are labeled "pooling" because each type of Sender takes the same action. The Sender's strategies of "cooperate if I am Genuine, defect if I am Pretender" and "defect if I am Genuine, cooperate if I am Pretender" are labeled "separating" because they prescribe different actions for each type.

Payoffs

Payoffs quantify interlocutors' preferences over the outcomes. Where do these preferences come from? A general reply is that they "emerge from social interactions in defending and opposing different ways of life;

shared values legitimating different patterns of social practices" (Wildavsky 1987: 5). In an interaction, they measure players' concerns about being marginalized and excluded by their communities while they are communicating with participants of other faiths in pursuit of common goals. These concerns ultimately relate to the interlocutors' social environments formed on their inclinations to interact with people and assessments of how people interact with them (Wildavsky 1987: 5). If one defects, this common pursuit with the other community is sacrificed to the concern of acceptance by co-religionists. If one "cooperates," one takes the risk of being criticized or excluded by one's own community but takes a step toward the common goal in cooperation with the other communities. Or, in Thomas Schelling's words, one obtains the value of a "meeting of minds" and "shared clues" (Schelling, 1960: 96).

The game contains eight outcomes: the first four stem from the actions of the Genuine and the other four result from the actions of the Pretender. This appraisal implies that there are 4! = 24 possible preference orderings for each type of the Sender and 8! = 40,320 orderings for the Receiver who evaluates, for example, whether mutual cooperation with the Genuine is preferable to mutual cooperation with the Pretender, and whether her unilateral defection in interacting with the Pretender is more valuable than the one in interacting with the Genuine and so on. To deal with this complexity, we will make preference assumptions based on players' ideas stemming from their presupposed prior experiences during the interaction since we cannot address each of these preference orderings.

Equilibria

Equilibria of asymmetric information games are labeled "Bayesian" because the uninformed player updates her beliefs via Bayes' rule about the type of player who moves first. There are four possible perfect Bayesian equilibria in the game. They are (1) "pooling on cooperation" where the player with superior information takes the same action so that both types cooperate; (2) "pooling on defection," which means that both types defect; (3) "separation" with the Genuine playing cooperation and the Pretender playing defection; and (4) "separation" with the Genuine playing defection and the Pretender cooperation (Gibbons, 1992: 186).

Pooling on Cooperation

Suppose that both the Genuine and the Pretender cooperate. The Receiver relies on her initial beliefs about the preferences of the Sender, as she gets no additional information about exactly which type has cooperated. Her initial beliefs about the Sender's type remain unchanged. We first propose a set of preferences for the Receiver to support the equilibrium. We assume that the Receiver prefers to reciprocate cooperation observing the Sender's cooperation. The Receiver could respond with defection, but that would end the dialogue.

As a result of the Receiver's reciprocation, the Genuine and the Pretender receive the payoffs of mutual cooperation. These payoffs are not equal as the Genuine and the Pretender evaluate mutual cooperation differently. Hence, to determine whether both types are really willing to cooperate, we need to specify how the Receiver would respond to deviation from cooperation to defection by the Genuine and the Pretender. There would be no pooling equilibrium were the Receiver to respond to any deviation that benefits one or both of them.

If the Receiver reacts to defection by cooperation, then the Genuine and the Pretender respectively earn their payoffs emanating from the Receiver's unilateral cooperation. We assume that the Genuine assesses mutual cooperation with the Receiver as more valuable than the Receiver's unilateral cooperation. The priority of the Genuine is supposed to be mutual agreement and cooperation. Hence, the Genuine would not deviate from cooperation to defection. As for the Pretender, he prefers the Receiver's unilateral cooperation gesture to mutual cooperation because he can increase his reputation in his community of being a "tough participant who defends the community's faith and beliefs" who has successfully elicited a compromise from the other side. Thus, the Pretender would deviate from cooperation to defection, were the Receiver to cooperate.

However, if we assume that the Pretender prefers mutual cooperation to the Receiver's retaliation against defection, the Pretender will stick to cooperation. Why would the Pretender regard mutual cooperation as preferable to mutual defection? One possible answer is that the Pretender prefers mutual cooperation to mutual conflict at this stage to achieve bigger gains at a later stage. The Pretender might also think that mutual defection will be perceived as a gross failure among peers compared to the gain that would be derived from the unilateral cooperation of the

Receiver. Therefore, the Receiver must reciprocate cooperation and retaliate by choosing defection against defection for both types to cooperate for the equilibrium to be established. Yet there is a problem: how would the Receiver know that the moves are coming from the Genuine or the Pretender?

The Receiver does not know whether defection comes from the Genuine or the Pretender when she observes defection. We assume that the spirit of dialogue prevails in the Receiver's mind when she believes that she is interacting with the Genuine. The Receiver would perceive the Genuine's defection as an exception to the norm, caused by extraordinary circumstances and would give him the benefit of the doubt. Thus, the Receiver prefers unilateral cooperation to mutual defection in her interaction with the Genuine. Yet if she believes that the defection is coming from the Pretender, she prefers to retaliate. She sees mutual defection as more rewarding and less costly than her unilateral cooperation in an encounter with the Pretender.

Which beliefs of the Receiver lead to her reaction to defect? The answer comes from the comparison of expected payoffs. The belief prompting the Receiver to retaliate is that it is somewhat unlikely that the defective move comes from the Genuine so that it is smaller than or equal to a specific ratio.[3]

Suppose that this belief condition is fulfilled. As the Receiver retaliates by choosing defection observing defection, the Genuine and Pretender obtain their mutual defection payoffs. The Genuine is assumed to prefer mutual cooperation to mutual conflict for the sake of a healthy dialogue, while the Pretender evaluates mutual cooperation as more preferable than mutual defection. The peer pressure the Pretender faces is in the direction of establishing superiority over the Receiver, not in the perpetuation of conflict. The Pretender thinks that future rounds of communication may offer opportunities to recruit the Receiver's unilateral cooperation anew. The Pretender then has an incentive to deviate from defection to cooperation given that the Receiver retaliates. The result is a perfect Bayesian equilibrium: pooling on cooperation.

Pooling on Defection

Let us suppose now that the Genuine and the Pretender both defect. The Receiver relies again on her initial beliefs about the Sender as she

---

[3] See Appendix 3 for the ratio and its computation from expected payoffs of the Receiver.

does not get any additional information about which type has defected. Her initial beliefs about whether she is interacting with the Genuine or the Pretender remain unchanged. We have already found that the Receiver's best response to defection is defection when her belief that defection comes from the Genuine is smaller than or equal to a specific ratio. If the Genuine moves to cooperation, the Receiver reciprocates as assumed. The Genuine then earns his cooperation payoff, which is higher than the payoff stemming from conflict with the Receiver. As a result, he prefers cooperation. The equilibrium then collapses.

If, however, the Receiver's belief that defection comes from the Genuine is higher than a specific ratio, then she still responds by cooperation. The Genuine is assumed to value mutual cooperation more than the Receiver's unilateral cooperation. Hence, he will deviate from defection to cooperation while the Pretender is happy with the unilateral cooperation of the Receiver. The pooling on defection equilibrium again collapses as the Genuine cooperates. Therefore, there is no pooling equilibrium in which both types defect.

Separation, with the Genuine Defecting and the Pretender Cooperating

When the Genuine defects and the Pretender cooperates, then the Receiver becomes certain that the one who cooperates is the Pretender and the one that defects is the Genuine. The Pretender obtains his mutual cooperation payoff as the Receiver reciprocates his cooperation. If he deviates to defection, the outcome will be mutual defection, something he seeks to avoid. Hence, he has no incentive to leave his equilibrium action. Yet the Genuine would deviate. The Receiver prefers to cooperate when she is certain that she is interacting with the Genuine. Thus, the Genuine earns the value of the Receiver's unilateral cooperation. As the Genuine evaluates cooperation with the Receiver more than the Receiver's unilateral cooperation, the Genuine would deviate from defection to cooperation. Thus, there is no perfect separating Bayesian equilibrium where the Genuine defects and the Pretender cooperates.

Separation, with the Genuine Cooperating and the Pretender Defecting

Similarly, when the Genuine cooperates and the Pretender defects, the Receiver becomes certain that the one who cooperates is the Genuine and the one that defects is the Pretender. As the Receiver prefers to reciprocate cooperation but retaliates against defection, the Genuine and the Pretender obtain their payoffs of mutual cooperation and mutual defection, respectively. It remains to check whether both the Genuine and the Pretender find their actions as optimal, given the replies of the Receiver. If the Pretender deviates to cooperation, then he obtains mutual cooperation, which he values more than mutual conflict. Thus, the Pretender has an incentive to deviate from defection to cooperation. As a result, there is no perfect separating Bayesian equilibrium where the Genuine cooperates and the Pretender defects.

Interpretations

The game implies conditions for successful interfaith dialogues deriving largely from a Receiver and the Genuine who has genuine intentions to communicate and find solutions to existing problems. Yet, the Receiver's interest in reaching out to others by cooperation is limited. She defects if she believes that the Sender prefers her unilateral commitment to strengthen his own reputation in his faith group. The Pretender's preferences are pivotal here, as even a slight change in those preferences would open new doors, leading to alternative equilibria. The Pretender hides his true intentions and waits for another round where he might reach his objective if the Receiver's unilateral cooperation is obtained. The Pretender pushes his luck to dominate the Receiver by not settling down with the status quo. Having a strong faith in a mutual understanding, the Genuine values mutual cooperation as preferable to any other outcome—to the extent of shunning the Receiver's unilateral cooperation. The Pretender, while he has an incentive to "show off" to his community, regards mutual cooperation as a better option than a failure of the communication through a mutual defection. Under different circumstances than those modeled in this game, he could possibly prefer a mutual defection, generating a separating equilibrium.

Our game assumptions imply how changes in the Pretender's mindset during the dialogue can produce a cooperative, successful interaction. The Pretender, even taking into account his prospective political gain, must be at a point to prefer reciprocated cooperation to mutual defection for a successful interfaith dialogue to occur. Similar to the Receiver, such a Sender type must have a sense of the worth of mutual cooperation, even though he is interested in his own reputation; otherwise, if the Pretender prefers mutual defection to cooperation, then separation— with the Genuine choosing cooperation and the Pretender defection—

becomes the only equilibrium. Thus, such a change in the Sender's preferences results in a shift in the equilibrium, implying a polarized communication with one group engaged in a genuine communication unlike the other.

More complicated interpretations are also possible. For example, one can evaluate cooperative moves either by the Genuine or the Receiver as related to motives of not being evaluated as selfish by others (Dana, Cain, & Dawes, 2006). Similar to the peer pressure, the Pretender is subject to, the Genuine and the Receiver might be coerced under group pressure to give in to cooperation. Thus, they might not genuinely care about the success of the dialogue, but they might be after a reputation of being collaborative.

We must also discuss the implications of the Receiver's belief threshold when she observes defection. The threshold gets progressively smaller and approaches zero if the Receiver evaluates the value of her unilateral cooperation and mutual defection in her interaction with the Pretender as being almost equivalent. In a sense, the Receiver does not evaluate these outcomes as being too different; they are almost equally attractive. Thus, under this condition and observing defection, the Receiver's inclination to think that defection emanates from the Pretender grows, prompting her retaliation. The Receiver's learning of the Sender's preferences during previous interactions or from other experiences is of utmost importance. The more often the Receiver encounters the Pretender and learns how participants in communication can pursue personal objectives rather than a genuine interfaith exchange, the smaller she will evaluate the difference between the value of mutual defection and that of a cooperative response to defection, and the more likely she will be to defect, with the belief that she is interacting with the Pretender.

The game provides valuable insights concerning interfaith dialogue, where participants remain uncertain about preferences. We have to decide which empirical traits can be evaluated as fruitful for further work on interfaith dialogue. We cannot derive universal statements from only one game model or a finite number of observations, but we are interested in sharpening our perspectives on what venues and perspectives provide possibilities in interfaith communication. Nor do we claim that all interfaith dialogues are in harmony with the game and its equilibria we propose. One can tell different stories to direct and enrich understanding of the observed interactions, as different interpreters' interests and prior beliefs can yield alternative assessments. It is possible to change payoff assumptions and deduce new equilibria that can enrich our insights through alternative readings and interpretations.

Next, we provide snapshots from a prominent case study of interfaith interactions during conflict, complementing our model of interfaith communications regarding the role of intentions and trust.

Snapshots of Interfaith Communications During Conflict: Northern Ireland

As a case study, we chose Northern Ireland against the backdrop of the "Troubles" from the late 1960s to the late 1990s. We do so since, despite a period of intense conflict and distrust, we could locate significant patterns of cooperation and interfaith communication that contributed to the 1998 Belfast Peace Agreement (Sandal, 2017). The "Troubles" is the name given to the period of intense conflict between the Loyalist segments (mostly Protestant) and the Republican segments (mostly Catholic) of the Northern Irish society between 1968 and 1998. The division arguably started in the early 17th century when Protestant colonists from Scotland and England took control over the local Gaelic and Catholic population and land. The Protestant community desired to keep the union with Britain whereas the Catholic population wanted autonomy. This dichotomy became especially violent, starting in the late 1960s and continuing until the 1998 Good Friday Agreement.

Although space limitations mean we cannot detail the causes and underlying dynamics of the conflict, scholars have pointed to competing ethnonational claims (McGarry and O'Leary, 1995), religious differences (Hickey, 1984; Bruce, 1994), colonialism (MacDonald, 1986) and economic inequality (Smith and Chambers, 1991) as possible sources for violence. The religious peacemaking efforts and communications in Northern Ireland were mostly "individualized" until the 1990s, in a manner where "personal motivation" interacted with "opportunities and constraints" on the ground (Brewer and Teeney, 2015: 3663).

Northern Ireland was not an easy environment to operate in as a peacemaker or a religious leader who wanted to engage in dialogue. Wells (2005: 11) notes that the level of distrust between the two communities was such that close to one-third of the Protestant adult male population in Northern Ireland were members of the Orange Order, which "requires adherents to strenuously oppose the fatal errors and doctrines of the church of Rome." In his recounting of the famous interfaith relationship between the Fitzroy Presbyterian Church and the Clonard Ministry, Wells (2005) emphasizes the level of personal friendship and trust between the church leaders (Ken Newell and Gerry Reynolds) and how the leaders agreed early on to assume a long-term view, "not ask too much too soon of their peoples" (p. 51), and how "even in the hard times of discouragement [...] they would always keep trying" (p. 106).

The remarks by Newell and Reynolds exemplify senders and receivers who are genuinely interested in mutual cooperation. Yet they would not erase any element of suspicion each side might have had about each other Wells' remark refers to. Given one-third of Protestants would likely reject any meaningful cooperation with the Catholics due to their belief system, this would affect how a Catholic leader would perceive any Protestant he might interact with. In general, when the two communities are engaged in a dialogue through two representatives, one can assume that either side might have suspicions about their preferences. The model also explains the absence of any interfaith communication with some political actors, such as the evangelical Ian Paisley. During the initial years of the Troubles, Church of Ireland Bishop Richard Hanson (1973) cautioned that

> "there are those in public life who style themselves ministers of religion and wear clerical collars, but who bring nothing of the message of religion to politics. They merely stand for a section of the Protestant community and only serve the identification with politics."

Under these conditions, it was to be expected that dialogue attempts between Ian Paisley and mainstream church leaders would fail, as church leaders did not trust Rev. Paisley's motives, and there was no common interest in sight that would make Ian Paisley prefer cooperation to mutual defection. Both Ian Paisley and the leaders of the four main churches (Roman Catholic, Church of Ireland, Presbyterian, and Methodist) like Richard Hanson signaled that they did not trust each other's motives and there were no common interests between Paisley and the other church leaders to make any communication meaningful.

Even in the interactions among the four main churches and their leadership, given the tensions and theological divisions, it was expected that the religious leaders would be wary of how efforts at interfaith communication would be received. Norman Taggart (2004:94), former President of the Irish Council of Churches and the Methodist Church in Northern Ireland, once averred that the church leaders did not want to be seen as reaching out to the other side and expressing an opinion on societal issues during the initial years of the Troubles, because "it was felt that this was the most effective and appropriate way of proceeding in the circumstances, on account of the suspicion in which ecumenism was held."

In such situations, as our model shows, looking tough becomes more important than sustained communications unless there are concrete common interests to work on. Hence, the initial successful examples of interdenominational cooperation during the Troubles—when religious leaders had yet to become familiar with each other's communication styles in a tense period of conflict—included functional and politically less sensitive issues such as housing, unemployment, and economic development. In instances where the participants are not sure of each other's motives and commitment levels, starting the communications with clear common goals will likely help even the leaders in the Pretender category who feel the need to consolidate their reputations within their own communities and lack an interest in a genuine understanding of the other.

Our model also maps out the balancing concerns about reaching out to the other versus remaining a representative of a tradition. "For generations," Gallagher and Worrall (1982:202) say, "Protestants were taught that Roman Catholic theology and devotion are unscriptural" and "Roman Catholics have been taught that Protestants were contumacious heretics destined for hell." In that sense, bold theological steps (despite the threat of protest from one's own community) taken by the sides were well received and created trust, and there were attempts to reciprocate, as our model would predict. For example, Protestant churches in Northern Ireland felt a need to revisit their centuries-old doctrines after the Second Vatican Ecumenical Council (1962) affirmed that an individual could be saved, regardless of his or her religious status. Given that "theological Protestantism and anti-Catholicism can lay claim to a longer unbroken historical pedigree in Ulster than any other still-existent ideological rival" (Morrow, 1997), it was challenging for the Protestant faith leaders to eschew hostilities without compromising their own religious identity. The Presbyterian assembly challenged a core document of the tradition, the Westminster Confession of Faith (1646), which regarded the Pope as "the Antichrist, the man of Sin, and the son of damnation." Delegates argued that this interpretation was not manifestly evident in Scripture. John Dunlop (1993), former leader of the Presbyterian Church in Northern Ireland, in a later speech recognized the importance of the Second Ecumenical Vatican Council in creating trust across the denominations:

> Since God cannot be privatized to only one of our two communities, or to the European Community of which our two countries are members, the challenge is to listen and speak across the frontiers and not to become the private chaplains of only one community. This has become easier since the end of Vatican II when the people in the churches are frequently now in frank discussion with one another.

In short, as the model shows, once actors see the genuine desire of the other side to reach out or to ameliorate relations, they are themselves more willing to engage in ambitious discussions and forgive instances of "defection" in individual interactions.

As the model also shows, for interfaith communications to succeed, the parties should either trust each other's motives or have common interests that require them to cooperate. A particular threat to a faith tradition might come from another tradition or from the establishment of a secular public sphere that excludes religious doctrines. For example, Cardinal Cahal Daly of Northern Ireland once stated that secularism is "more anonymous and more subtle than either Nazism or Communism were" as a threat to faith (quoted in *The Irish Times*, 2000). This common "threat" posed by secularism fits into the model of what game theorists call "the dilemmas of common aversions," when "actors with contingent strategies do not most prefer the same outcome but do agree there is at least one outcome that all want to avoid" (Stein, 1982:309). In other words, the leaders of two different faith traditions might cooperate to prevent a secular order from taking hold of the public sphere.

Obviously, not all interfaith arrangements aim to find faith-based solutions to replace secular arrangements. Some patterns of interreligious cooperation would fit better with "dilemmas of common interests," in which all actors prefer a given outcome, such as environmental protection or eradication of hunger. One factor contributing to the consolidation of ecumenical activities and a more rigorous faith-based agenda of conflict resolution in Northern Ireland was the increasingly secular approach to public issues. The secular arrangements created competition by posing an alternative perspective for disillusioned members of society and endangered religious leaders' prestige. Therefore, in several instances, religious leaders stated that their greatest concern was secularization rather than challenges posed by "the other." Rev. Patrick McCafferty (1997) stated that

> the opinions of anti-Catholic extremists do not reflect the beliefs of the vast majority of our Protestant fellow-Christians in Northern Ireland. We must be united in our common witness for the truth against the real enemy: the forces of nihilism, hedonism, secularism, and godlessness.

Although Northern Ireland's population retained its reputation as one of the most "religious" communities in Europe, the level of practice had fallen during the late 1980s and early 1990s (*Irish News*, 1991). Methodist President Norman Taggart (1998), for example, stated the importance of religion in the public sphere: "We today need relevant visions arising from our own circumstances. Political Protestant and political Catholics, secular Catholics and secular Protestants need to be truly converted to Christ." The Bishop of Derry and Raphoe, James Mehaffey (1997), urged church leaders to take a more active role in stamping out sectarianism: "People will demand to know and to be informed. Advances in the information technology field will need to be matched by far greater openness and by effective channels of information within the churches and outward to society." Trevor Morrow (2000), Moderator of the Presbyterian Church, commented that a combination of consumerism and individualism meant the church is treated more like a restaurant or supermarket "than as an essential expression of a person's identity." The Catholic Bishop of Clogher, Joseph Duffy, and his Church of Ireland counterpart, Bishop Michael Jackson (both quoted in *Belfast Telegraph*, 2007), also stated that the Irish people needed to reassess their values, and holidays like Christmas provide an opportunity to do this. They claimed that "society has suffered due to a slide toward secularism, and there is currently great anxiety about a loss of the sacred" (ibid). As predicted by our model, such common goals as increasing the overall interest in religion can bring religious leaders together in interfaith initiatives even if they have no knowledge of each other's levels of credibility and trustworthiness.

Conclusion

Interfaith interactions involve asymmetric information, expectations, and levels of trust. Religious actors enter interreligious communication for different purposes as rational actors. We use two ideal types in our model: (1) a participant who is interacting with "the other" because he believes this is the right thing to do in pursuit of a common goal and is not vulnerable to pressure from his own community, and (2) a participant who interacts with the other but is highly influenced by reputational concerns and peer pressure, and wants to use interfaith communication to further his own political standing. Our model shows that a positive outcome is possible in both scenarios, although some outcomes are preferable to others in the long term. Although some of the insights -especially the ones related to reputational concerns- can be applied to other communications that involve ethnic and racial identity, the model we use is most helpful to further understand the dynamics of interfaith interactions.

According to our model, for interfaith communications to be successful, the participants must fulfill two criteria. First, religious actors should clearly prefer mutual cooperation to mutual defection and conflict, which requires them to have a clear common goal. Even if one participant prefers a scenario where the other party is cooperative while herself remaining defiant for reputational purposes, as long as she values a mutual solution/cooperation to mutual defection/conflict, the interfaith interaction will likely be successful.

Second, trust matters. The parties will be more tolerant of defiant-looking behavior if they believe they are dealing with a partner who is sincere and not prone to peer pressure, rather than one who cares more about his reputation than the communication itself. That is why it is critical for parties to the interfaith interaction to convey their genuine interest in dialogue and make clear that they are not vulnerable to external pressure. Bishop Cahal Daly (1989) once recommended that "Catholic seminarians and Protestant candidates for the ordained ministry should have opportunities for joint contact and discussion and, where possible, shared sessions and seminars." Such points of contact and iterated interactions can help with successful interfaith communications and interactions even in times of conflict.

In this study, we modeled a particular type of interfaith interaction and we do not claim that our model's insights are relevant to every single interfaith scenario. There has been no scholarly attempt to systematically model different interfaith communication scenarios. Therefore, to our knowledge, this is one of the very first steps toward understanding the parameters of interreligious interactions. Although game theory is used in almost every sphere of international relations theory and political science, it is surprisingly underutilized when it comes to interfaith communication. Further development of research and models will be helpful to understand interfaith interactions under additional constraints and conditions. We encourage taking more advantage of the game theoretical models to investigate dynamics of cooperation and conflict among the religious actors. Future research agenda in this respect should address the multiple reasons why religious actors -with various priorities and values- participate in organizations, rituals, and other initiatives with insights into their concerns and interests. Interfaith communications, as this paper has shown, will continue to be a topic of interest for future scholars of game theory. Any investigation that includes religious leaders' and organizations' public relations concerns can also be part of this research agenda.

References

Abu-Nimer, M., Khoury, A. and Welty, E. (2007). Unity in Diversity: Interfaith Dialogue in the Middle East. Washington, D.C.: United States Institute of Peace.

Bender, C. and Cadge, W. (2006). "Constructing Buddhism(s): Interreligious Dialogue and religious hybridity", *Sociology of Religion*, 67 (3): 229-247.

Brewer, J.D. and Teeney F. (2015). "Violence, tolerance and religious peacebuilding in Northern Ireland", *The Changing World Religion Map*. Dordrecht: Springer.

Bruce, S. (1994). The Edge of the Union: The Ulster Loyalist Political Vision: The Ulster Loyalist Political Vision. Oxford: Oxford University Press.

Bunza, M.U. (2016). Challenges of Muslim-Christian relations in Nigeria. In: E.K. Chia (ed.), Interfaith Dialogue. New York: Palgrave Macmillan.

Cartwright, N. (2010). Models: Parables v. Fables. In: R. Frigg and M.C. Hunter (eds.) Beyond Mimesis and Convention: Representation in Art and Science. Dordrecht: Springer.

Cilliers, J. (2002). Building bridges for interfaith dialogue. In: D. Smock (ed.) Interfaith Dialogue and Peacebuilding. Washington, DC: United States Institute of Peace.

Cornille, C. (2013). Conditions for interreligious dialogue. In: C. Cornille (ed.) The Wiley Blackwell Companion to Interreligious Dialogue. Malden, MA: Wiley.

Daly, C. (1989, 25 January). "Bishop Tells Clergy to Stay Out of Politics," Irish News.

Day, J. (2021). "Everyday Practices of Toleration: The Interfaith Foundations of Peace Accords in Sierra Leone". Politics and Religion, 14 (1): 54-82.

Dana, J, Cain, D, and Dawes, R. (2006). "What you don't know won't hurt me: Costly (but quiet) exit in dictator games", Organizational Behavior and Human Decision Processes,100 (2): 93–201.

Devitt, M. (1997). Realism and Truth. Princeton: Princeton University Press.

Duffy, J. (2007, 19 December). "Bishops Criticize Increasing Secularism in Irish Society," Belfast Telegraph.

Dunlop, J. (1993). Christianity and Politics in Northern Ireland. Belfast: St. Thomas' Parish Church.

Fletcher, J.H. (2007). "As long as we wonder: Possibilities in the impossibility of interreligious dialogue", Theological Studies, 68 (3):531-554.

Friedman, M. (1953). Essays in Positive Economics. Chicago: University of Chicago Press.

Gallagher, E. and Worrall, S. (1982). Christians in Ulster, 1968-1980. NY: Oxford University Press.

Geertz, C. (1973). The Interpretation of Cultures. New York: Basic Books.

Gibbons, R. (1992). A Primer in Game Theory. New York: Harvester, Wheatsheaf.

Gopin, M. (2002). Holy War, Holy Peace: How Religion can Bring Peace to the Middle East. NY: Oxford University Press.

Habel, P. and Grant, J. (2013). "Demand for God and Government: The Dynamics of Religion and Public Opinion", Politics and Religion, 6 (2):282-302

Haddad, Y.Y. and Fischbach R. (2015). "Interfaith dialogue in Lebanon: Between a power balancing act and theological encounters", Islam and Christian–Muslim Relations, 26 (4):423-442.

Hanson, R. (1973, 23 March). "Clerics in Politics Attacked," Belfast Telegraph.

Hickey, J. (1984). Religion and the Northern Ireland Question. Dublin: Gill and Macmillan.

Iannaccone, L.R. (1994). "Why strict churches are strong", American Journal of Sociology, 99 (5): 1180-1211.

Iannaccone, L.R. (1995). "Voodoo economics? Reviewing the rational choice approach to religion", Journal for the Scientific Study of Religion, 34(1): 76–89.

Irish News (1991, 21 January). Survey shows one in four have no interest in religion.

Jackson, M. (2007, 19 December). Bishops criticize increasing secularism in Irish society. Belfast Telegraph.

Jelen, T.G. (2001). Notes for a theory of clergy as political leaders. In: E.S. Crawford and L.R. Olson (eds.) Christian Clergy in American Politics. Maryland, Baltimore: The Johns Hopkins University Press.

Jervis, R. (1976). Perception and Misperception in International Politics. NJ: Princeton University Press.

Kadayifci-Orellana, S.A. (2013). "Inter-religious dialogue and peacebuilding". In C. Cornille (ed.) The Wiley-Blackwell Companion to Inter-Religious Dialogue. NJ: John Wiley & Sons.

King, S.B. (2011). Interreligious dialogue. In: C. Meister (ed.) The Oxford Handbook of Religious Diversity. NY: Oxford University Press.

Kyaw, N. N. (2019). Interreligious Conflict and the Politics of Interfaith Dialogue in Myanmar. Singapore: The Institute of Southeast Asian Studies (ISEAS).

Kolvenbach, P. and Pittau, J. (1999). Understanding and Discussion: Approaches to Muslim-Christian Dialogue. Rome: Editrice Pontificia Universita Gregoriana.

Laustsen, B. and Wæver, O. (2000). In defence of religion: Sacred referent objects for securitization. Millennium 29 (3): 705-739.

Lederach, J.P. (1995). Preparing for Peace: Conflict Transformation Across Cultures. Syracuse, NY: Syracuse University Press.

MacDonald, M. (1986). Children of Wrath: Political Violence in Northern Ireland. Cambridge: Polity Press.

Malik, A. (2013). "Reconciliation between Muslims and Christians: Collective action, norm entrepreneurship, and 'a common word between us'", Journal of Religious Ethics, 41(3): 457-473.

McCafferty, P. (1997, 22 April). "The theology of hatred", Belfast Telegraph.

Mehaffey, J. (1997, 14 August). "Churches must take lead to stamp out sectarianism: Mehaffey". Belfast Telegraph.

Morrow, D. (1997). "Suffering for righteousness sake? Fundamentalist Protestantism and Ulster politics". In: P. Shirlow and M. McGovern (eds.) Who Are "The People"?: Unionism, Protestantism, and Loyalism in Northern Ireland, London: Pluto Press.

Morrow, T. (2000, 17 June). "Stability will mean emptier churches", Belfast Telegraph.

Neufeldt, R.C. (2011). "Interfaith dialogue: Assessing theories of change", Peace & Change, 36 (3): 344-372.

O'Leary, B. and McGarry, J. (1995). Explaining Northern Ireland: Broken Images. Oxford: Blackwell.

O'Neill, B. (2001). Honor, Symbols, and War. Ann Arbor: The University of Michigan Press.

Orton, A. (2016). "Interfaith dialogue: Seven key questions for theory, policy and practice", Religion, State and Society, 44 (4): 349-365.

Perica, V. (2001). "Interfaith dialogue versus recent hatred: Serbian Orthodoxy and Croatian Catholicism from the Second Vatican Council to the Yugoslav War, 1965-1992", Religion, State and Society, 29 (1): 39-66.

Putnam, R.D. (1988). "Diplomacy and domestic politics: The logic of two-level games", International Organization, 42 (3): 427-460.

Riitaoja, A.L. and Dervin, F. (2014). "Interreligious dialogue in schools: Beyond asymmetry and categorisation?", Language and Intercultural Communication, 14 (1): 6-90.

Sandal, Nukhet A. (2017). Religious Leaders and Conflict Transformation: Northern Ireland and Beyond. New York: Cambridge University Press.

Schelling, T. (1960). The Strategy of Conflict. Cambridge, MA: Harvard University Press.

Scott, T. (2000). "Taking religious and cultural pluralism seriously: The global resurgence of religion and the transformation of international society", Millennium, 29 (3): 815-841.

Smith, D.J. and Chambers, G. (1991). Inequality in Northern Ireland. Oxford: Oxford University Press.

Sosis, R. and Alcorta, C. (2003). "Signaling, solidarity, and the sacred: The evolution of religious behavior", Evolutionary Anthropology, 12:264-274.

Stein, A. (1982). "Coordination and collaboration: Regimes in an anarchic world", International Organization, 36 (2):299-324.

Taggart, N. (1998, 17 March). "Church Leaders Hopeful of Talks' Success," Belfast Telegraph.

Taggart, N. (2004). Conflict, Controversy and Cooperation: The Irish Council of Churches and 'The Troubles', 1968-1972. Dublin: Columba Press.

Takim, L. (2004). "From conversion to conversation: Interfaith dialogue in post 9-11 America", The Muslim World, 94: 343-355.

Twiss, S.B. (2018). Explorations in Global Ethics: Comparative Religious Ethics and Interreligious Dialogue. NY: Routledge.

Vüllers, J. (2021). Mobilization for peace: Analyzing religious peace activism. Conflict Management and Peace Science, 38(4): 391-410.

Wells, R. (2005). Friendship Towards Peace: The Journey of Ken Newell and Gerry Reynolds. Dublin: Columba Press.

Wildavsky, A. (1987). "Choosing Preferences by Constructing Institutions: A Cultural Theory of Preference Formation", American Political Science Review, 81 (1): 3-22.

Young, L.A. (Ed.) (1997). Rational Choice Theory and Religion. London: Routledge.

Appendix 1

Pooling on Cooperation

If $r\ U^R(O_4) + (1-r)\ U^R(O_8) \geq r\ U^R(O_3) + (1-r)\ U^R(O_7)$, playing D is optimal for the Receiver observing D. If we solve the inequality for r under these assumptions, we obtain the Receiver's belief condition to play D following D:

$$r \leq \frac{U^R(O_8)-U^R(O_7)}{U^R(O_8)-U^R(O_7)+U^R(O_3)-U^R(O_4)}.$$

Assume that r satisfies the above weak inequality condition. As the Receiver plays D against D under this condition, the Genuine obtains $U^1(O_4)$ and the Pretender obtains $U^2(O_8)$ if both types shift from C to D. We assume that $U^1(O_1) > U^1(O_4)$ and $U^2(O_5) > U^2(O_8)$. Therefore, we obtain a perfect Bayesian equilibrium pooling on cooperation denoted as:

$$[\{C, C\}, \{C, D\}; r \leq \frac{U^R(O_8)-U^R(O_7)}{U^R(O_8)-U^R(O_7)+U^R(O_3)-U^R(O_4)}]$$

Pooling on Defection

Suppose that both types defect. Bayes' rule implies that $r = p$. We have already found that the Receiver's optimal response to defection is defection if:

$$r \leq \frac{U^R(O_8)-U^R(O_7)}{U^R(O_8)-U^R(O_7)+U^R(O_3)-U^R(O_4)}$$

Suppose that the belief condition holds. Thus, the Genuine obtains $U^1(O_4)$ and the Pretender obtains $U^2(O_8)$. If the Genuine deviates to C, the Receiver responds by C, therefore earning $U^1(O_1)$. We have $U^1(O_1) > U^1(O_4)$ by assumption. So, there is no pooling equilibrium in which the Sender plays $\{D, D\}$. However, if $r \geq \frac{U^R(O_8)-U^R(O_7)}{U^R(O_8)-U^R(O_7)+U^R(O_3)-U^R(O_4)}$, so that the Receiver responds to defection with cooperation, the Genuine obtains $U^1(O_3)$. Given assumption $U^1(O_1) > U^1(O_3)$, the Genuine has an incentive to deviate from D to C. Consequently, there is no pooling on D equilibrium.

IN THE INTERSECTION OF RELIGION, IDENTITY, AND EDUCATION: THE PERCEPTIONS OF SUNNI MUSLIM PARENTS REGARDING ISLAM COURSES IN AUSTRIA

Ece Cihan Ertem[1]

Introduction

The Muslim population in Austria grew significantly in the second half of the 20th century due to immigration from countries such as Turkey and Bosnia and Herzegovina. Much of this population change was the result of guest worker immigration from Turkey to Austria, as well as a product of civil war in former Yugoslavia. According to the statistics of the Ministry of Foreign Affairs of Austria, the country has a Muslim population of about 335,000 people who hail from various countries including Turkey, Bosnia and Herzegovina, Iran, Egypt, Syria, Iraq, Lebanon, and India. The majority of these Muslims are of Turkish origin, constituting 134,210 people, followed by Bosnian and Herzegovinian Muslims, the number of which is reported in official statistics at 96,214. Furthermore, there are between 20,000 and 30,000 Muslims from other countries. The ministry states that the majority of the Muslim population in Austria is Sunni, accounting for about 85 to 90 percent, while about 10 to 15 percent are Shiites, including Iranians, Alevites, and some Kurdish minorities. However, it is essential to note that the Muslim population in Austria includes both immigrants who have received Austrian citizenship and native Austrians who have converted to Islam (Hafez, et al., 2005).[2]

Being the most populous Muslim minority group, there have been various reasons for Turkish citizens to migrate to Austria since the 1960s.

---

[1] Dr. Ece Cihan Ertem, University of Vienna, Vienna, Austria.
[2] Austrian state also denotes that these numbers belong to the census of 2001, after it stopped collecting data on religious affiliation via censuses. Therefore, the Austrian state denotes that "there are no current numbers of members of religious communities represented in Austria recorded by the state", itself. (https://www.oesterreich.gv.at/themen/leben_in_oesterreich/kirchenein___austritt_und_religionen/3 /Seite.820018.html) However, religious communities also officially published statistical estimates based on their membership numbers. According to this data, the number of Muslims in 2016 was around 700,000 and therefore Islam would be the second largest denomination in Austria after Catholic Christianity.
(https://www.oesterreich.gv.at/themen/leben_in_oesterreich/kirchenein___austritt_und_religionen/3 /Seite.820018.html)

In the context of Turkish-Austrian relationships, the term *"Gastarbeiter"* (a German term literally translates to "guest worker") has been mostly used within the literature describing Turkish citizens who came to Austria as migrant workers starting from the 1960s and 1970s, mainly in response to the post-WWII economic boom in European countries including Austria and the labor shortage at the time. These Turkish citizens were brought to Austria as temporary workers, with the expectation that they would eventually return to Turkey. However, many ended up settling in Austria and building families, becoming permanent residents, and contributing to the country's economy and society (Gürses, Kogoj, Mattl, 2004; Yağmur & Vijver, 2022; Wetts, 2006; Woschitz, 2021).

The Muslim community in Austria is an integral part of the country's rich cultural heritage and their rights were officially recognized by the Austrian state earlier than in many other European countries (Kolb, 2020). In public secular primary schools in Austria, Islamic religious education has been provided since 1982 (Tuna, 2020; Aslan &Windisch, 2012). These lessons are designed to teach children about Islam, its history, and traditions in order to promote mutual understanding and respect between persons of different religious and cultural backgrounds. Despite being generally appreciated, there have been many theoretical discussions about Islamic religious education in Austria concerning the teaching methods, professionalization of teachers, teacher education, curricula, and the context of secular schools. (Kramer, 2021, pp.255-257; Kolb, 2021, p.5; Aslan, & Hermansen, 2021.)

Even though the Turkish community in Austria is largely engaged in the activities of religious education for their children, there have not been many studies based on the impressions of Turkish parents or analysis of the discourse of Turkish educational policies for the Turkish diaspora. (Some exemplary works could be listed as but not limited to Çitak, 2018, Kroissenbrunner, 2003; Maritato, 2018; Scheibelhofer, 2007). Hence, this paper focuses on the Islam courses that Turkish migrant children in Austria attend, and aims to analyse the findings of the conducted research on the thoughts and impressions of Turkish Sunni parents regarding Islam lessons in schools and Quran courses in mosques in the country. The paper not only covers the existing literature on the literature but also aims to shed light on the topic via qualitative research based on the data from fieldwork recently conducted in Austria. While scrutinizing the topic, it is important to note that, within this research, the term "Turkish" is used as an umbrella term to refer to individuals of different ethnic backgrounds living in Turkey. One can assume that the Turkish Sunni community followed only Islamic courses for their children, however, after the literature review and first couple of interviews, it is easy to notice that the Turkish community also prefers having non-Islamic religion lessons as well. Hence the initial research questions are revised and listed accordingly as follows:

- Do Turkish parents want their children to have religion lessons at schools and what are the reasons for their preferences?

- Do Turkish parents need extra religion lessons (such as courses in mosques or at several other platforms) other than the ones at schools?

- What do Turkish parents living in Austria think about existing Islamic lessons (both at schools and other platforms)?

- Last but not least, what is the meaning and/or importance of religion lessons for Turkish parents living in Austria?

This paper includes a literature review of the research subject including the recent educational policies of the Austrian government vis-à-vis Islam education, an analysis of the contemporary documents regarding Quran education of Turkish migrant children in Austria, and the results of parent interviews. To scrutinize the subject, qualitative methods are followed. In addition to document analysis, 10 semi-structured parent interviews were conducted in person and online; in the Turkish language then translated into English. As a Turkish expatriate, born and raised in Istanbul, also having Istanbulian parents, the researcher had not had any direct relationships with the sample group which mostly migrated from different cities or urban areas of Anatolia. Therefore, it was a major challenge for the researcher since she lacked any networks while reaching the sample group. Furthermore, she does not belong to the religious Muslim population in Turkey and thus does not wear/carry any objects/clothes that would signify any belonging to any religious group. These factors made it difficult to access the interviewees who are found via the snowball method by which participants were recruited through referrals from initial participants. Since the snowball method is often used when studying hard-to-reach populations, such as those who are stigmatized or marginalized, it would be relevant and beneficial to conduct research on the Turkish Sunni

Muslim community in Austria with this method. As well as being a hard-to-reach population, some members of the sample group believe that they are not totally marginalized but stigmatized and discriminated against by several means in Austrian society as to be discussed in the conclusion part of this paper; which makes the sample group suitable for the chosen methodology.

The research process began with the researcher identifying a small number of initial participants via the academic environment of the University of Vienna. Participants were then asked to refer other potential participants who meet the study's inclusion criteria. By establishing trust and rapport with participants who were being referred by someone they know and trust, the researcher was able to access 10 female interviewees between the ages of 25-45 and living in and outside of Vienna. There are several reasons why all participants are female. The snowball method allowed the female researcher to access the female participants more since mothers were more connected to each other via parental groups. Secondly, since the researcher is also female, it allowed female participants to talk to her in a more relaxed manner which could be relevant to the Muslim-Turkish culture. Thirdly, even though the researcher looked for fathers to talk to within the sample groups, mothers were more responsive and for many families, mothers were the first contact person regarding school issues. As a last point for the methodology of the research, it would be relevant to denote that, just like many other works, this research has limitations as well. Due to time constraints, only Sunni Turkish parents are interviewed. For further studies, it would be illuminating to look at the preferences of Alevi families as well. Furthermore, this research only comprises female participants whereas interviewing fathers could also contribute to the research. A possible multiplication in the number of participants would create a broader understanding of the topic. Due to the diverse nature of the Turkish immigrant community, more participants from different districts of Vienna and different cities of Austria would be valuable in order to portray differences regarding social stratification and perspectives on religion.

Islam Courses in Austria- A literature review and background information

The literature review of this paper seeks to analyse the history, current state, and future developments of Islam courses in Austria by looking at existing research on the subject and providing an overview of the most relevant findings. The rights of the Muslim community have been recognized in Austria by the enactment of the Islam Law (known as its German name in the literature, *Islamgesetz*) decreed in 1912. *Islamgesetz* was a set of laws passed in Austria to regulate Muslim activities in the country. The main provisions of this law included the recognition of Islamic holidays, the establishment of Muslim burial grounds, and the appointment of imams to lead religious services. This law aimed to protect the rights of Muslims in Austria, while also providing them with an opportunity to practice their faith without fear of persecution or discrimination. The Islam Enactment of 1912 was repealed in 2015, although its main provisions are still observed today. (Hunt, 2002; Mattes and Rosenberger, 2015; Eberwein, 2019) The 2015 Act was severely criticized by some scholars stating that it paved the way for unjust treatment and led to discrimination against the Muslim population in Austria (Dautović and Hafez, 2019; Sezgin, 2019; Sauer 2022). The part of the act banning foreign funding for Islamic organizations (https://www. bundeskanzleramt.gv.at/en/agenda/integration/the-austrian-islam-law.html) has changed the practice of the courses conducted at mosques since many of the imams, who are the main educators of Quran courses at mosques, have been recruited and financed by Turkey's head of religious affairs, the *Diyanet*. This ban has been discussed in the media and was mentioned by interviewee (discussed in the upcoming sections), since it directly affected the situation of Imams teaching children at mosques.

Within the framework of public education by the Austrian state, Islam lessons in Austria are officially conducted in primary, secondary, and high schools, taking place in a one hour course for primary schools and two hours for high schools. These courses are designed to teach children about Islam, its history, and traditions in order to promote mutual understanding and respect between different religious and cultural backgrounds. At the primary school level, students are taught about the Five Pillars of Islam, the Prophet Muhammad, and Islamic etiquette. Classes can also focus on more in-depth topics such as Islamic law, and some of them are designed to further promote understanding and mutual respect between different cultures. (Kolb 2021; Sezgin, 2019)

Furthermore, Islam courses can also take place in mosques throughout Austria within the legal framework of Quran reciting courses. These classes cover a wide range of topics, from the basics of Islam to more advanced topics such as Islamic legal theory and the history of Islamic civilization. The classes are often led by experienced Imams and are open to both Muslims and non-Muslims alike. Like the Islam lessons in schools, these classes in mosques have been largely well-received, with Turkish immigrant children in Austria typically learning Islam through a combination of religious education at home and local mosques or Islamic community centres. Many parents encourage their children to attend weekly classes or workshops where they can learn about the principles and practices of Islam, as well as its history and cultural traditions. There are also summer schools, excursions, camping, and sports activities also organized by the mosques where Muslim children can participate within the framework of Quran courses. (https://imameoesterreich.univie.ac.at/en/imams-in-austria/associations-and-mosques/index.htm)

In addition to formal religious education, Turkish immigrant children may also learn about Islam through observing and participating in religious practices within their families and communities. For example, they may attend Friday prayers at the local mosque with their parents, participate in Ramadan observances and other religious festivals, and learn how to pray and perform other Islamic rituals. Mosques have started offering courses for both adults and children on topics such as the Qur'an, religious law, Islamic traditions, and ethics. Mosques also organize regular events such as lectures and seminars, often focusing on topics related to interfaith dialogue, Islamophobia, and other issues affecting the Muslim community in Austria. Mosque administrators often work closely with their local governments and civic organizations to ensure that their services are properly integrated with the larger Austrian society. They also serve as a platform for dialogue between Muslim and non-Muslim citizens, which can help foster a more harmonious society (Hafez, et al., 2005).

There are several institutions involved in the topic of Turkish migrants in Austria and Islam lessons and these are also frequently mentioned by the participants during the interviews. The most general Islamic institution related to the research subject is the Islamische Glaubensgemeinschaft in Österreich (IGGiÖ) [Islamic Religious Community in Austria]. The IGGiÖ was established as a body incorporated under public law in 1979 to provide legal representation to Sunni/Hanafi Muslims living in Austria. In 1912, only the Hanafi school of thought was recognized, primarily for Muslims from Bosnia and

Herzegovina. However, in 1979, all Sunni schools of thought and Shiite groupings, including Twelver Shi'a, Zaidites, and Ibadites, were acknowledged. The Turkish-Islamic Union for Cultural and Social Cooperation in Austria (*Avusturya Türk Islam Kültür ve Sosyal Yardımlaşma Birliği*, ATIB) has been the formal representative of the largest group of Sunni Turkish Muslims, since 1991. It was established as a semi-state representation of the Turkish Head of Religious Affairs (Diyanet) which has dealt with religious issues of Muslims from Turkey since the 1970s (Hafez, et al., 2005). According to their mission statements, ATIB strives to promote understanding and integration of the Turkish-Muslim community in Austria. The organization organizes a range of activities such as language courses, sports activities, and social events. Additionally, ATIB also provides advice and support to the Turkish Sunni community on topics such as education, housing, and legal matters (www.atib.at).

Muslim immigrants to Austria have also organized themselves based on the organizational statute, forming mosque organizations that reflect various ethnoreligious and ideological trends of Islam. In the documents prepared by the Ministry of Foreign Affairs, it is stated that the plurality of the Islamic community in Austria, concerning countries of origin, languages, cultural and religious traditions, etc., has challenged the comprehensive representation claims of IGGiÖ in all religious issues. Nonetheless, most organizations actively participate in IGGiÖ or have come to terms with it. (Hafez, et al., 2005) Even though IGGiÖ is recognized as an umbrella organization by the state, the Alevi community in Austria is represented by various different associations. One of them is the *Alevitische Glaubensgemeinschaft in Österreich* (also known as ALEVI, Alevi Faith Community in Austria) is one of the organizations for the Alevi community in Austria. The Austrian Alevi Islamic Faith Society (ALEVI) was accepted as the official representative organization of the Alevi community in 2013 and remained the legal Alevi representative organization in the educational area until 2022. As of 2022, a new group within the AABF, which took the name of the Free Alevi Faith Community (Frei-Alevitische Glaubensgemeinschaft in Österreich) which was initially only referred to as a "state-registered religious denomination" (Religiöse Bekenntnis gemeinschaften) category in Austria, gained the status of legal recognition. This group defined itself as a unique belief group, not within Islam. In addition to the Free Alevi Faith Community and ALEVI, mostly founded by Kurdish citizens, the Old Alevi Belief Community in Austria (AAGÖ) also exists in Austria since 2013 (Cosan Eke, 2023).

Interviews with Turkish Parents and Findings from the Research

This research utilized a qualitative methodology, conducting 10 semi-structured interviews and adopting the thematic analysis method to examine the data. The thematic analysis allowed for a comprehensive and in-depth understanding of the data by identifying patterns and themes rather than simply counting word frequency. Several key themes that the analysis revealed could be listed as follows but not limited to a) general impressions and expectations of Turkish parents regarding religion lessons in Austria, b) preferences of parents about religion lessons, c) factors influencing these preferences, and d) evaluations and criticisms from Turkish parents on religion lessons. To maintain anonymity, all interviewees were assigned randomized letters. The interviews were conducted in Turkish. The participants were either born in Turkey or had parents from Turkey.

a) General Impressions and Expectations of Turkish Parents about Religion Lessons in Austria

This section of the article is linked to the first and second research questions of this paper. According to the data gathered from the fieldwork, all Turkish parents that have been interviewed have decided to send their children to religion lessons either at school or another platform. However, during the pre-field work period of this research, I also met Turkish parents living in Austria whose children do not have any religion lessons. This study does not focus on this group, but this topic is open to further research and might be conducted as a continuation of the current research.

Turkish parents in Austria had expectations and pre-assumptions before sending their children to religion lessons. One of the parents AZ (randomly coded letters for anonymity) who is an academic herself says that the Islam education offered in schools is mostly related to the ethics of Islam and provides general knowledge on the Islam religion. AZ has two kids, a daughter (15) and a son (8), and did not go to mosques to get a Quran education herself even though she identifies herself as a "faithful Muslim." She had some hesitations about sending her kids to mosques at first but then decided to send her daughter to Quran education when she was in the 3rd grade:

"We did not want our children to have a strict religious education, an education that might scare children from Hell for example. During our childhood, some friends of mine who are now in their thirties had such Quran courses which I think affected them in a reverse way, they might be being distanced towards religion now. However, we wished our children to recite Quran and we did not have time to teach them. That's why we sent them to summer schools in mosques in cooperation with *Islamisches Zentrum Wien.* The Quran lessons there are in German and there is an international environment there, children are from different ethnicities. She had a wonderful summer they did not only learn Quran but also had some ethics lessons, moral rules, some words of Prophet Mohammed, etc. As far as I could observe the quality of courses and educators are on the highest level, they are very careful about teaching methods/pedagogy."

As could be seen from the quote, parents think that the Islamic education at school might not be sufficient for learning details of Islam and they need a comprehensive education on Quran reciting, the Arabic alphabet, and more details about religion. Another parent EL describes impressions about and expectations from the Islamic courses as follows:

I wish children to go to Islam courses at schools however if there are not enough [registered] kids, there are no Islam courses. It is so dangerous, really. I call many mothers and even send them, please, if you don't send your children the courses will be closed. Mothers argued that children don't learn anything or they always learn the same thing…and also my son, for example, finishes his lesson at 1 o'clock at noon on Wednesdays, two or three hours later, that is, at 4 o'clock there is an Islam lesson. He has to go back to school again. Now the thing is getting a teenager back to school…after arriving at home…is difficult afterward. There is nowhere to wait and three hours in winter, let's say it's ok in summer, it's easy and simple to spend time with friends [...]. But what will he do in winter? ... If the Austrians' religion lesson is the first lesson in the morning, It's very simple actually.

Just like this parent, many other parents denoted that Islam courses are given in the afternoons, a couple of hours later than the other classes finish. This issue has made children not attend Islam courses since many of them do not want to come back to school after they arrive home.

Parents note that it should not be that difficult to schedule Islam courses in the morning just like Catholic courses have already been scheduled in the mornings. Some of them think that this educational policy is a purposeful one aiming to diminish the number of students taking Islam courses. Since Islam courses at schools are closed when the student number is below the pre-designated threshold, they find this afternoon class policy quite discriminatory.

Another point that was emphasized by the parents is about the registration policies for Islam courses at schools. EV, an academic and a mother of four underlined the fact that in her daughter's school, there had been no Islam courses since the day they registered her, all the Islam courses were closed due to the "insufficient number" of Muslim students. EV describes her perspective on the issue as follows:

> "I've noticed that some teachers are making great efforts to get students unenrolled from the Islamic course. When children are already enrolled in school, you inform them which religion they belong to, according to him, the school already knows from the beginning. At the beginning of the year, we say head teachers said to our daughter constantly, "You have to remove yourself, so you have to deregister. Why is that? Because you don't attend the Catholic class." Yes, but she is not enrolled in the Catholic class, that Muslim is enrolled in the Islamic class. … You can cancel your registration for the Islam class, then don't enroll in any religious classes. There is such a thing because every group of Islam has the legal status here like other religions, that is, every Muslim child has the right to take such a course while going to public school or going to public school. But if the child removes himself from that record, he does not have to go to those classes. For some reason, this was the thirteenth Vienna school, a lot about it. Because until today, until the day when the daughter of that house started school, there was no Islamic lesson in the building of that school."

There is a much scholarly literature emphasizing that the Turkish community does not find Austrian society particularly welcoming and friendly, with the phrase "discrimination" having been pronounced often in this context (Baysu, Phalet and Brown, 2014; Dogan and Strohmeier, 2020; Goreis, Urs, and Mewes, 2021; Wanka, et al., 2019; Weichselbaumer, 2015). Furthermore, Turkish parents think that the education system in Austria is not inclusive enough and their children feel discriminated especially due to the selectiveness of the education system. The assessments on German language skills just after 4-year primary school education, which is essential in the education path (whether leading to Gymnasium or types of vocational school at such an early age), had led to immigrant communities being excluded from academic education (Baysu and De Valk, 2012; Schnell and Fibbi, 2016; Song, 2011; Söhn and Özcan, 2006). My fieldwork also reinforces this perspective. Several participants have mentioned that they have faced discrimination during their own educational path as well and have been concerned that their children will face the same attitude. EV explains her thoughts on this point as follows:

> This is something that has to start, of course, with teacher training first. Teachers receive little to no training on this subject. Be it in PH, the first teachers are trained in PH, and gymnasium teachers are trained here at the university. "How can I greet this diversity?" They have no such preoccupation, both in the sense of their education and occupation, but also... even in the sense of a more humanistic perspective. Austria is not just a place full of ethnic Germans,[3] especially Vienna. In other words, there are statistics here in Vienna, the background of 50% of Vienna is of immigrant background. There is a 70-80% immigrant background, especially in primary schools. The teachers, however, still feel as if they are dealing with a homogeneous German ethnic and German-speaking group, unaware of the fact that they are dealing with a heterogeneous group, whether cultural or religious. Even if they are aware, they just think...you know... they think they have to teach without questioning and thinking on these issues... Then they try to put children into this mould, and when children do not fit into this mould, the child becomes a problem. Then he finds many syndromes in the child, let it be ADHD, etc.

b) Preferences of Parents for Religion Lessons in Austria

Turkish parents living in Austria have neither the same religious beliefs and practices nor similar preferences regarding the decision on their children's religious lessons. Some parents do not prefer to send their

---

[3] By the word "German "in this quote, the participant means "Austrian" and German people. In the interviews, it is also seen that participant used the term "German" as a counterpart to "Austrian" in contexts of population and language. As it was explained in introduction of this text, all the interviews were held in Turkish and translated to English of which the researcher herself is a certified translator in between these two languages.

children to any religion courses whereas some Muslim parents prefer to send their children to other religious courses such as Catholic ones. One of my interviewees IL, who is an academic living in Austria for more than 10 years and the mother of a 7-year-old, notes that both she and her Austrian husband are Muslims, but they send their children to Islam courses neither at school nor at the mosque. She explains their decision of sending their children to a Catholic course as follows:

> Since my son has Islam in his religion section, they [his school] assigned him to the Islamic course automatically. However, we wanted him to learn all religions, and when we talked to the class teacher at the school, the teacher said, if you want something like that, then I recommend that you start with Roman Catholic, because our Catholic teacher tolerates world religions like that. Hence, we thought about that, and it made sense. We met the Catholic religion teacher. She is a really sweet woman. We could not meet the Islam teacher because he did not show up at the parent-teacher day. Then we gave a petition saying that our child leaves the Islam class and attend the Catholic religion classes. We might reconsider our decision again next year and send him to Islam courses as well.

With this quote, it is also seen that the content of Islam courses and the impression of Islam teachers over parents are also important in parental decisions. The same parent also denoted that some religious Muslim parents might send their children to even private Catholic schools rather than public schools and regular Islam courses provided by them:

> My friend [religious Muslim] sent all three of his children to Catholic school. There are a lot of Turkish children in the region where they live, in 10th Vienna. There is a very large Turkish population in schools, especially in the schools closest to them, and there are too many Turkish children. Therefore, the children in those schools spoke Turkish and she said that they want their children's German comprehension to not decline or improve, so they sent them to Catholic schools to get a better education. This friend of mine is also a teacher in public schools. In other words, since she knows the system very well, what the children go through, and the schools very well... In 10th Vienna, there are many problems and complaints by parents about schools, many

families are not satisfied. But conscious families are trying to keep their children away from those schools in order to provide a better education opportunity [for their children]. My friend is one of them, so she sent her children to a Catholic school. In that region some families are not qualified, you know, those who are not well-educated, low-paid jobs, and therefore cannot have time to take care of their children very well"

This quote also underlines the fact of inequality among the schools located in different parts of the city. The 10th district of Vienna called *Favoriten* is a region where mostly immigrant families live. There are many works written on district-based inequality among schools in the Austrian system and the above quote also implies that parents belonging to middle or upper classes avoid public schools and Islam courses where children would hear the Turkish language most of the time. On the contrary, some parents deliberately prefer these schools and Islam lessons because they would help their children to improve their Turkish. In the upcoming section, I would elaborate on the reasons why some parents prefer Islam courses.

c) Factors Determining the Choice of Turkish Parents on Islam Religion Courses

According to the fieldwork, one of the most effective factors for Turkish parents to send their children to Islam courses at school and mosques is parental wish to protect their native culture, identity, and language. There is a variety of motivations for Turkish parents in Austria to send their children to Islam courses. According to the data from fieldwork, the first and foremost motivation is the preservation of cultural and religious identity. Interviewees noted that they want to ensure their children maintain a connection to their cultural and religious heritage, even if they are living in a foreign country. By sending their children to Islam courses, parents feel that they are helping them to understand and appreciate their Turkish and Muslim identity.

Since we live together for many years, I find it quite weird that discrimination towards us still continues... I see it, especially among teachers at school...For many years there have been *Gastarbeiters* in this country living together with Austrians. For example, some Austrians find it strange that we are still Muslims... I'm thirty-seven years old, I was born here. I'm used to their religion, Christianity, I know when *Weihnachten* is, how it happens, and when it ends. But they still have such a prejudice [on Ramadan] for example and they may still be surprised when I fast. They have little knowledge about our religion. .. I wear a hijab. When I go out, their first approach to me is, since I'm wearing a hijab, they don't speak German... they talk to me, but they talk as if I cannot understand German... When I start talking, they are startled. As I said... It stems from Austrian national education.

Some parents believe that it is important for their children to receive a formal religious education in order to understand and practice their faith. They believe, Islam courses can provide children with a deeper understanding of the religion and help them to develop a stronger bonding with their community. Furthermore, sending children to Islam courses also serves as a way for Turkish families to become more connected to other Turkish families and the wider Muslim community in Austria. This helps them to feel more at home and can provide children with a sense of belonging.

Last but not least, language acquisition is an important factor for Turkish families when sending their children to Islam courses. The lack of Turkish courses at Austrian public schools hinders Turkish children in acquiring their native tongue and parents denoted that, among other reasons, they send their children to mosques to enable them to practice their native tongue. As one parent stated, "We send our children to these courses not only to deepen their religious understanding but also to enable them to practice and maintain their native tongue".

d) Evaluations and Criticisms of Turkish Parents for Religion Lessons in Austria

Many Turkish parents welcome Islam courses at schools and mosques however they also have criticisms of the way courses are conducted. As denoted above there were several criticisms of the Austrian school system, but in this section, we will focus on the criticism of the curricula and pacing of the courses. These criticizing group of parents are mainly religious Muslim parents and would like Islam courses to be improved. The criticisms are mainly constructive and deal with both the organization of the courses (including state regulations) and teaching aspects.

One parent UL, who is also an Islam religion teacher at a public school denoted that it would be better if the educators at mosques would have a pedagogical perspective towards children, she was worried that children might feel away from religion if they are treated in an entertaining pedagogical manner:

> It is very nice to have religious education in mosques, but there are many shortcomings. Unfortunately. You know, the heart desires that people who have a real pedagogical education give the Islamic lesson or people who understand a little more about the language of children. There is an understanding in mosques, you know, whoever has good religious knowledge can give lessons, you know. In no way do they look at his character or his thing, they don't look at what education he's had. People who do not understand the language of the child behave this way and I feel sorry for how they will explain Islam. The children get cold after that, they don't want to go to the mosque.

Another parent, AZ denotes that some teachers at the mosque could be judgemental towards girls' clothes and attitudes and might approach the students in a more conservative way than their families do. However, she also stated that teachers are collaborative when parents state their concerns about these issues:

> We are Muslim Austrians. That's how she [her daughter] knows her identity, be a Muslim, but be an Austrian Muslim. Her cousin and she like to wear trousers and don't wear skirts when they leave. My daughter observed that a teacher looked at her cousin in a judgemental way since she wore trousers. Not quite sure though. I said, is it okay? I said the teacher was very wrong if she judged the students. If that teacher puts his religious education in the foreground, it should not be a problem for her. But that's what we need to talk about, sometimes with children. We live in such a society that, for example, transgender is a category and you have to respect that, too. One more thing caught my attention. For example, we sing like this in the car when we go somewhere or... they asked for a hymn, so I sang a hymn. I opened it from someone who says, lady. She was Bosnian. "Do you know, mother?" said E. I wouldn't expect it at all because I'm trying to raise my daughter as a feminist. He says, in fact, the female voice is haram. But I said E, I said we listen to songs too. I said, what do you mean haram? Who said that? I said look, we have sister F in this congregation, she is a hafiz. He is reading the Quran everywhere. He also sings

the melody. I said if it was haram, he wouldn't do it. I said that, in such a society, at such a time, who will be affected by that female voice? That's what I said, that's ridiculous. I said, men cannot determine this, I said to whom and what is haram. When you do things like this, tell me so we can talk.

The term "Austrian Muslim" is a captivating one and an eye-opening category for this work since in present literatüre, the term used is usually "Muslims of Austria" or "Muslim Austrians" referring to the religious identity of the minority community (Hödl, 2010; Kroissenbrunner, 2003; Meixner, Friedl, and Hartl, 2018). Contrary to the previously cited literature, the findings of this research show that some participants define themselves as "Austrian Muslims" more often than Turkish Muslims. "Austrian Muslim" is a phrase that signifies the unification of these two concepts. The participants actually point out an adaptation and an integration process into Austrian society. They define a situation of having elements of these two cultures, rather than a stereotypical image of first-generation guest worker life, and with the concept of "Austrian Muslim," they distinguish themselves from the existing conservative segment of Muslim society in Austria.

Conclusion

This research conveys Turkish parents impressions of Islam courses in Austrian schools and mosques. It seems that the Turkish Muslim Sunni community has quite diverse thoughts on Islamic education and cannot be simply reduced to several definitions and understandings of the religion. While some Sunni parents send their kids to Muslim religion courses, some might prefer Catholic courses, and some of them might wish to have homeschooling. This research has shown that the Turkish Muslim community is not homogeneous or monolithic in Muslimhood even though they have perceived like that. Some Muslim parents send their children to Catholic schools or Catholic lessons whereas others think that there should be more Islam classes in school for their children.

There are different reasons why parents send or do not send their children to Islam courses. According to the findings of the fieldwork presented here, preservation of cultural and religious identity are identified as the primary motivations for Turkish parents in Austria to send their children to Islam courses. Parents express a desire to protect their native culture, identity, and language by providing their children with religious education and instruction in the language and customs of their home country. As one interviewee put it, they want to ensure that their children maintain a connection to their cultural and religious heritage, even if they are living in a foreign country. By sending their children to Islam courses, parents feel that they are helping them to understand and appreciate their Turkish and Muslim identity.

Many Turkish parents in Austria see formal religious education as a crucial aspect of the upbringing of their children. They believe that attending Islam courses can provide children with a deeper understanding of their faith and help them to develop a stronger connection to their community. Additionally, these courses serve as a way for Turkish families to become more connected to other Turkish families and the wider Muslim community in Austria, which can help children feel a sense of belonging. Furthermore, language acquisition is also an important consideration for Turkish parents when deciding to send their children to Islam courses. Due to the lack of Turkish courses offered at Austrian public schools, parents see these courses as an opportunity for their children to practice and acquire their native tongue.

Furthermore, many parents see mosques as social places for their children. Looking at the diverse data gathered from semi-structured in-depth interviews, it can be concluded that mosques and Islamic youth organizations serve as social places for Turkish children in Austria in a variety of ways since these platforms provide a space for children to connect with other Turkish children and families, fostering a sense of community and belonging. Many parents noted that children play together at mosques and/or after religion courses and mosques host events and activities that bring together Turkish children and families, such as youth groups, sports teams, and cultural celebrations. Besides, mosques are described as venues serving as a hub for language and cultural classes, where Turkish children can learn about their heritage and practice their native language. Even though there is criticism towards Islam courses at mosques, the majority of the interviewees believe that mosques can provide a space for children to explore and express their identity, particularly since they are struggling to navigate the cultural differences between their neighborhoods, traditions, and Austrian mainly Catholic traditions. Despite this struggle, the concept of Austrian Muslim identity was often uttered during the conversations. Several parents stated that their children, all were born in Austria, have an Austrian Muslim identity as an umbrella concept that signifies a bond that is beyond a nationalist perspective. These parents wish their children to learn Islam in German and have the capacity to discuss controversial issues about Islam in German.

Some parents stated that they experience discrimination when Islam courses and their daily Islam practices are considered. There are several statements among the fieldwork data regarding the feelings of Turkish parents in Austria that their children are experiencing discrimination regarding Islam courses at schools. Many parents observed that Islam courses at public schools are scheduled after regular class hours and therefore their children do not want to wait for these afternoon classes that are a couple of hours later than other classes Furthermore, at schools there are no places for these children to wait for Islam courses. Some parents stated that their children would be the first ones to attend Islam courses at their school and sometimes their teachers asked them to withdraw from Islam courses. These practical issues caused Turkish parents to feel that their children are being stigmatized or discriminated against because of their Muslim identity and that this is reflected in the way Islam is taught in schools. Finally, parents realized that recent political issues such as the relationship between Austria and Turkey and the change in the political discourse between these two countries also paved the way for these discriminatory actions. While the Islam Act of 2015 changed the law regarding foreign funding for religious activities, it also created discrepancies related to Turkish imams serving at Austrian mosques. Participants noted that this led to a lack of the number of imams as educators, as well as the recruitment of only retired imams at Austrian mosques since imams were not allowed to get a salary from Turkey with the changed law. Furthermore, literature in this context discusses the regulatory measures that were taken to control and monitor specific immigrant target groups in Austria, especially after 2017 (Gruber and Rosenberger, 2021; Perchinig and Valchars, 2019). For example, the government program of 2017-2022 in Austria redefined "Political Islam" by announcing a bill aimed to prohibit it and founding a center to observe and fight against it. These plans were not implemented before the government collapsed in 2019, but they were taken over by the coalition government in 2020. Furthermore, some mosques accused of extremism and illegal foreign funding were also shut down and these actions were perceived as strict control by Muslim populations in Austria (Gruber and Rosenberger, 2023).

In conclusion, this paper has contemplated the concepts of religious minority groups, identities, and discrimination at the intersection of politics and education by focusing on the specific case of the Turkish Sunni Muslim population in Austria and the Islam courses that to which they send their children in Austria. After the analysis of the data and the findings of the conducted research inspecting the thoughts and impressions of Turkish Sunni Muslim parents on the topics, it is relevant to say that the Turkish Sunni Muslim community has a lot to say about this topic, and members of the community often expressed their disappointment with the policies regarding Islam courses at schools and mosques. In accordance with the literature, research participants also underlined the rise of right-wing governments in Europe that has led to judgemental attitudes towards Muslim daily practices and cast a shadow on the ideal of the diverse, democratic culture of Austria. Last but not least, this subject is open to further studies with fieldwork by scholars in order to promote equality, diversity, and inclusion of minorities in Austrian society.

References

Abid, Lise Jamila. "Muslims in Austria: Integration through participation in Austrian society." *Journal of Muslim Minority Affairs* 26.2 (2006): 263-278.

Aslan, Ednan, and Marcia Hermansen, eds. *Religious Diversity at School: Educating for New Pluralistic Contexts*. Springer Nature, 2021.

Aslan, Ednan, and Zsófia Windisch. *The Training of Imams and Teachers for Islamic Education in Europe. Wiener Islamstudien. Volume 1*. Peter Lang GmbH, Internationaler Verlag der Wissenschaften. Eschborner Landstrasse 42-50, D-60489 Frankfurt am Main, Germany, 2012.

Baysu, Gülseli, and Helga De Valk. "Navigating the school system in Sweden, Belgium, Austria, and Germany: School segregation and second-generation school trajectories." *Ethnicities* 12.6 (2012): 776-799.

Baysu, Gülseli, Karen Phalet, and Rupert Brown. "Relative group size and minority school success: The role of intergroup friendship and discrimination experiences." *British Journal of Social Psychology* 53.2 (2014): 328-349.

Cosan Eke, Deniz. 2023. "Avrupa´da Alevilerin Dünü ve Bugünü". In Sükrü Aslan, Cigdem Boz, Cemal Salman, *Sosyal Bilimler Perspektifinden Aleviler ve Alevilik 1*. Istanbul: Ütopya Yayinevi.pp: 167-202

Çitak, Zana. "National conceptions, transnational solidarities: Turkey, Islam, and Europe." *Global Networks* 18.3 (2018): 377-398.

Dautović, Rijad, and Farid Hafez. "Institutionalizing Islam in contemporary Austria: a comparative analysis of the Austrian Islam act of 2015 and Austrian religion laws with special emphasis on the Israelite act of 2012." *Oxford Journal of Law and Religion* 8.1 (2019): 28-50.

Doğan, Aysun, and Dagmar Strohmeier. "The role of discrimination, acculturation, and ethnic identity in predicting psychosocial functioning of Turkish immigrant youth." *Contextualizing immigrant and refugee resilience: Cultural and acculturation perspectives* (2020): 99-122.

Eberwein, Martina. *Das neue Islamgesetz 2015-eine juristische Bewertung/eingereicht von Martina Eberwein.* Unpublished Dissertation, Universität Linz, 2019.

Gruber, Oliver, and Sieglinde Rosenberger. "Between opportunities and constraints: right-wing populists as designers of migrant integration policy." *Policy Studies* 44.2 (2023): 155-173.

Goreis, Andreas, Urs M. Nater, and Ricarda Mewes. "Protocol: Effects of chronic ethnic discrimination in the daily life of Turkish immigrants living in Austria: study protocol of a 30-day ambulatory assessment study." *BMJ Open* 11.10 (2021).

Gürses, Hakan, Cornelia Kogoj, and Sylvie Mattl. " Gastarbeiter. 40 Jahre Arbeitsmigration [Guest workers. 40 years of labor migration]." (2004).

Hafez, S. *et al.* (2005) *180 Degrees East and West: Muslims in Austria, in their homelands, and living together in the new Europe.* rep. Vienna, Austria: Federal Ministry for Foreign Affairs of the Republic of Austria.

Hafez, Farid. "Debating the 2015 Islam law in Austrian Parliament: Between legal recognition and Islamophobic populism." *Discourse & Society* 28.4 (2017): 392-412.

Hafez, Farid. "Institutionalized Islamophobia: The Draft of the Austrian Islam-Law." *Seta Perspective* 14 (2014): 2-4.

Hödl, Klaus. "Islamophobia in Austria: the recent emergence of anti-Muslim sentiments in the country." *Journal of Muslim Minority Affairs* 30.4 (2010): 443-456.

Hunt, Robert. "Islam in Austria." *The Muslim World* 92.1/2 (2002): 115-.

Kramer, Michael. "Islamic Religious Education in Austria and Its Challenges for the Social Integration of Muslim Pupils." *Religious Diversity at School.* Springer VS, Wiesbaden, 2021. 253-273.

Kolb, Jonas. "Constituted Islam and Muslim Everyday Practices in Austria: The Diversity of the Ties to Religious Organizational Structures and Religious Authorities in the Process of Change." *Journal of Muslim Minority Affairs* 40.3 (2020): 371-394.

Kolb, Jonas. "Muslim diversity, religious formation, and Islamic religious education. Everyday practical insights into Muslim parents' concepts of religious education in Austria." *British Journal of Religious Education* (2021):

Kogelmann, Franz. "Germany and Austria." *Islam Outside the Arab world* (1999): 315-336.

Kroissenbrunner, Sabine. "Islam and Muslim immigrants in Austria: socio-political networks and Muslim leadership of Turkish immigrants." *Immigrants & Minorities* 22.2-3 (2003): 188-207.1-14.

Mattes, Astrid, and Sieglinde Rosenberger. "Islam and Muslims in Austria." *After integration.* Springer VS, Wiesbaden, 2015. 129-152.

Maritato, Chiara. "Addressing the blurred edges of Turkey's diaspora and religious policy: Diyanet women preachers sent to Europe." *European Journal of Turkish Studies. Social Sciences on Contemporary Turkey* 27 (2018).

Meixner, Oliver, Raphael Friedl, and Barbara Hartl. "Preferences for attributes of halal meat: empirical evidence from the Muslim community in Vienna, Austria." *International Journal on Food System Dynamics* 9.1012-2018-4124 (2018).

Religionsgemeinschaften in österreich – statistik (no date) *oesterreich.gv.at - Österreichs digitales Amt.* Available at: https://www.oesterreich.gv.at/themen/leben_in_oesterreich/kirchenein___austrit t_und_religionen/3/Seite820018.html (Accessed: February 3, 2023).

Sauer, Birgit. "Radical right populist debates on female Muslim body-coverings in Austria. between biopolitics and necropolitics." *Identities* 29.4 (2022): 447-465.

Scheibelhofer, Paul. "His-stories of belonging: Young second-generation Turkish men in Austria." *Journal of intercultural studies* 28.3 (2007): 317-330.

Schnell, Philipp, and Rosita Fibbi. "Unequal Pathways. School-to-Work Trajectories for Children of Turkish and Western-Balkan Origin in Switzerland and Austria." *Swiss Journal of Sociology* 42.2 (2016): 266-290.

Sezgin, Zeynep. "Islam and Muslim minorities in Austria: Historical context and current challenges of integration." *Journal of International Migration and Integration* 20.3 (2019): 869-886.

Song, Steve. "Second-generation Turkish youth in Europe: Explaining the academic disadvantage in Austria, Germany, and Switzerland." *Economics of Education Review* 30.5 (2011): 938-949.

Söhn, Janina, and Veysel Özcan. "The educational attainment of Turkish migrants in Germany." *Turkish Studies* 7.1 (2006): 101-124.

"Startseite." ATIB Union, www.atib.at. (Accessed: February 3, 2023)

Tuna, Mehmet H. "Islamic religious education in contemporary Austrian society: Muslim teachers dealing with controversial contemporary topics." *Religions* 11.8 (2020): 392.

Wanka, Anna, et al. "Everyday discrimination in the neighbourhood: What a 'doing'perspective on age and ethnicity can offer." *Ageing & Society* 39.9 (2019): 2133-2158.

Weichselbaumer, Doris. "Discrimination against migrants in Austria: An experimental study." (2015).

Wets, Johan. "The Turkish community in Austria and Belgium: The challenge of integration." *Turkish Studies* 7.1 (2006): 85-100.

Woschitz, Johannes. "Attitudes towards Turkish and Turks in Austria: From Guestworkers to "Quasi-Foreigners" in a Changing Social Landscape." *Languages* 6.1 (2021): 58.

Yagmur, Kutlay, and Fons JR van de Vijver. "Socio-cultural, Demographic, Educational and Linguistic Characteristics of Turkish Abroad." *Multidisciplinary Perspectives on Acculturation in Turkish Immigrants*. Springer, Cham, 2022. 13-38.

ALEVISM AS A POLITICAL-THEOLOGICAL CONCEPT AND ITS REPRESENTATION IN AUSTRIA

Deniz Cosan Eke[1]

In recent years, the impact of migration on religion and religious communities has been frequently discussed in connection to the construction of migrants' identities. According to Gallo (2014), these debates are perceived as a threat to national identity and so religious communities are increasingly politicized by national governments. These debates have affected not only those who migrate, but also those who live with immigrants in their countries of origin, and lead to further discussion of political, economic, legal, and cultural implications, as well as to inter-religious dialogue and intra-faith diversity (Henkel & Knippenberg, 2005[2]; Gallo, 2014[3].

Like the diversity that exists between different religions, the diversity within the same religion can be so varied that it is difficult to find a singular definition of that religion. For example, Sunni and Shia Muslims or Catholic and Protestant Christians define their respective denominations differently but are able to place for themselves within the same religion despite having internally divergent beliefs and rituals.

Recently, religious diversity in Europe has been attempted at the institutional level through a process of recognizing religious groups within their legal rights. However, such religious diversity at the institutional level has led to debates about the representation of faith rather than the creation of a pluralistic structure. Representation in the religious context is a complex issue, but one of the most difficult aspects of representing a religion or faith is that the spiritual nature of that faith and the cultural tradition of that faith group is regulated by those who have the right to legal representation. The purpose of this chapter is to draw attention to the impacts and consequences of representations of a faith on religious groups and organizations by examining the

---

[1] Deniz Cosan Eke, University of Vienna, Vienna, Austria.
[2] Henkel, Reinhard and Hans Knippenberg. 2005. "Secularisation and the Rise of Religious Pluralism: Main Features of the Changing Religious Landscape of Europe." In Hans Knippenberg, ed. The Changing Religious Landscape of Europe. Amsterdam: Het Spinhuis: 1–13.
[3] Gallo, Ester (ed). 2014. Religion and Migration in Europe: Comparative Perspectives on South-East Asian Experiences. Farnham, Surrey: Ashgate.

representation of a religion from an insider's perspective.

Alevism is often discussed as a different interpretation of Islam because most Alevis do not fulfil the "five pillars of Islam" as part of their religious rituals and do not go to mosque. Briefly, these five conditions to be Muslim are: *Shahada* (Faith) means that the statement of faith in one God (Allah) and His messenger and it is the first requirement of becoming a Muslim. *Salah* (Prayer) is the ritual prayer required of every Muslim five times a day throughout their lifetime. *Zakat* (Almsgiving) refers to the obligatory donation that consists of a Muslim giving a portion of his wealth to those in need during his lifetime. *Sawm* (Fasting) is the act of fasting during the one month (Ramadan) during his life. The requirement of *Hajj* (Pilgrimage) means that every Muslim should visit to Mecca as a sacred place at least once in their lifetime if it is within their means.

Instead of these religious rituals, the main religious rituals of the Alevis are *cem*, and the place of worship is called *cemevi*. The *Cem* ritual is performed at least once a year. Men and women pray in the same place and Alevi clergy (*dede* or *ana*) address the members of the congregation as *Canlar*, meaning "pure soul," which can also be expressed as an emphasis on gender equality in the *Cem* rituals. Music and ritual dance, i.e., the *semah,* are important parts of Alevi religious practice, as is eating together afterwards. Another important difference from Sunni Islam is that women can be religious leaders in Alevi rituals.

The definition of Alevi religious identity has been influenced for many years by the socio-political conditions in Turkey, the Alevi homeland. Alevis living in Turkey have often hidden their Alevi identity until recently because their practice differs from the majority Sunni Islamic groups, and many have been afraid of political and socio-cultural pressures. Although Alevism is still not officially defined as a faith in Turkey, the number of people who publicly identify themselves as Alevis has increased in recent years. Correspondingly, Alevis began organizing in the 1990s for more representation and equal opportunity.

The migration experience has contributed to Alevi awareness not only of other faiths but also of internal diversity among Alevis. Like all religious groups in European countries, Alevis who have migrated to Europe are divided into different groups in terms of rituals and group dynamics due to political, legal, social, and cultural differences affecting each country in which they live. For this reason, there are various definitions of Alevism that we frequently encounter both in the literature and especially at the organizational level. The most notable of these definitions is that, hile the differences in religious practice between Alevi and Sunni groups are discussed by most Alevis in Turkey with the claim that Alevism is the essence of Islam."[4] Among most Alevis in the diaspora these differences have reinforced the debate that Alevism is a faith separate from Islam[5].

In this chapter, Alevis—the religious and cultural group whose definitions are often debated in terms of whether they should be represented within or outside Islam—are included in the framework of representation of religious groups, diversity and religious pluralism. Austria has been chosen as an exemplary European country to both reflect on the paradoxical developments regarding Islamic groups and to inform on the contentious dimensions in Alevi communities. Methodologically, data collection was done through literature research and news about Alevi and Alevism in Austrian media channels, and through Alevi associations web pages. The study specifically focuses on a research question: How is Alevism experienced and represented in Austria? This research question has been answered with the issues explained in three sections. First, I provide a review of the current debates of Alevism within its political and theological dimensions. Second, I explore the impacts of migration on Alevis and Alevi organizations. Third, I illustrate the theological and political orientation of Alevi Associations and the representation of Alevis in Austria. In the light of this background, this chapter will contribute to the debates in the context of theology and politics that have been gaining attention in recent decades.

Alevism with its political and theological dimensions: What is Alevism

Alevism is a faith that has been shaped as a unique religious and cultural identity in Turkey, and which has spread to many countries through transnational migration processes. Different estimations exist on the figures of the Alevi population. But the population of Alevis is approximately 15% to 20% of Turkey's total population. There are Kurdish, Turkish, and Arab Alevis in Turkey. Alevism has not been

---

[4] 'Alevilik mezhep değil, asıl İslam'ın özüdür' (t24.com.tr) (retrieved on 22.06.2021)
[5] Sökefeld, Martin. 2005. Integration und transnationale Orientierung: Alevitische Vereine in Deutschland. In Karin Weiss &Dietrich Thränhardt (hrgs). SelbstHilfe. Wie Migranten Netzwerke knüpfen und soziales Kapital schaffen. Freiburg: Lambertus Verlag. Pp: 47-68.

officially recognized by the Turkish state because state policies have supported the creation of a Turkish Sunni national identity after the 1982 Constitution.[6] Alevi faith maintains local and regional differences, but it is possible to state that Alevism is still the second-largest faith groups in Turkey after Sunni Muslims.

Alevism includes a rich historical origin, different cultural codes, and traditions, so it is difficult to rigidly define. Nevertheless, the definitions for Alevism across various studies are as follows: First, Alevism is a religious affair and an interpretation of Islam. The essence of Islam within Alevism is defined by loyalty to Ali, the descendant of Imam Ali. In some sources, Alevism is described as the love for Imam Ali, who is the cousin and the law-in-son of Prophet Muhammed, and for the sons of Imam Ali.[7] Because of the relationship and kinship between the Prophet Muhammad and Imam Ali, the debate remains as to whether Alevism stands inside or outside Islam. Secondly, Alevism offers a political philosophy of freedom and resistance against injustice. Thirdly, Alevism essentially represents a culture and a way of life, covering different religions and cultures (Bilici, 2005).[8]

In short, as stated by Kosnick (2004), "Despite the shared historical roots, Alevi belief developed in a separate direction, drawing upon sources of Turkish mystical Islam and Anatolian folk culture."[9] However, nationalism, religion, culture, minority status, immigration, and citizenship have led to different definitions of Alevism in local, national, and transnational contexts. In fact, it can be argued that these debates reflect a search for a positioning for the Alevi faith. If one analyzes this positioning desire of many Alevi Associations in Turkey and Europe with the method of discourse analysis, it can be seen more as a reflection of ideological concerns and of a demand for political identity formation than as a theological definition. On the other hand, these different interpretations, perspectives, and practices, which can also be seen as an

---

[6] Coşan Eke, Deniz. 2021. "The Changing Leadership Roles of Dedes in the Alevi Movement .Ethnographic Studies on Alevi Associations in Turkey and Germany from the 1990s to the Present". Bielefeld: Transcript.

[7] Büyük Dinler Tarihi Ansiklopedisi İslamiyet, Hıristiyanlık, Musevilik ve İlkel Dinler, 1976; Osmanlıca-Türkçe Ansiklopedik Büyük Lûgat, Abdullah Yeğin vd, 1997; Osmanlıca-Türkçe Ansiklopedik Lûgat Eski ve Yeni Harflerle, Ferit Develi Oğlu, 2000; Türk İnönü Ansiklopedisi, 1948-1980: Cilt II; Türk Dili ve Edebiyatı Ansiklopedisi (Devirler, İsimler, Eserler, Terimler), 1977- 1998: Cilt 1.

[8] Bilici, Faruk.2005. "The Function of Alevi-Bektashi Theology in Modern Turkey." In *Alevi Identity: Cultural, Religious and Social Perspectives*, edited by Olsson, Tord, Özdalga, Elisabeth, and Raudvere, Catharina, 59–73. London: Routledge.

[9] Kosnick, Kira. 2004 "Speaking in One's Own Voice: Representational Strategies of Alevi Turkish Migrants on Open-Access Television in Berlin.". *Journal of Ethnic and Migration Studies*. 1 September 2004. Vol. 30, No. 5.

expression of the depth of Alevism, show that this faith needs further theological study. To provide a general framework for those who have little or no knowledge of the Alevi faith, it would be good to give a brief information from the theological background of the Alevi faith.

In Alevi cosmology, God is also called *"Hak"* or the Truth that created life. Alevis believe that there is no separation between God and the world created by him, because the universe here is the emanation of the divine substance itself. In this sense, strictly speaking, the Alevi doctrine does not know a creator God, but the creation as a component of the Divine, so that the created world reflects His Being.[10] The universe represents God, and there is no God in the universe defined differently from what exists.

Alevism as a faith manifests itself as both a communal faith, based on collective rituals and a personal spiritual existence that aims to reach perfection. According to Alevi belief, man is the same substance as God, that is, man is an image of God and God shows his creativity through human being. But, if a person can reach a point that transcends his own ego, his self, then he can be a real part of the whole. This transcendent point is defined as the perfect man. The aphorism of Hacı Bektaş-i Veli,[11] who is the most important saints in Alevism reads "the greatest book to be read, is the human being," and is often used by Alevis to explain their understanding of religion. Briefly, Alevism can be summarized with the statement of Adolf von Harnack, "It is to man that religion pertains."[12] because Alevism incorporates the tradition of the "man-centered theology" (Schleiermacher, 1996).[13]

Alevis share reverence for Imam Ali, a son-in-law of the Prophet Muhammed, and his descendants, whom they regard as the Prophet's only legitimate successor. In addition to this, they believe in the unity of God, the Prophet Muhammad, and Imam Ali. But this is not defined as the state of being three or trinity, like in Christianity (God, Christ, and the Holy Spirit). It is rather that the Prophet Muhammad and Imam Ali are representations of God's light and (not of God himself), being neither independent from God, nor separate characteristics of him (Sözer,

[10] http://www.aleviten-krefeld.com/Glaube.html
[11] *The Bektashi Order of Dervishes.< bektashiorder.com>*. (retrieved on 21.06.2021).
[12] von Harnack, Adolf. What Is Christianity? Thomas Bailey Saunders, trans. (Philadelphia: Fortress Press, 1986), 8.
[13] Schleiermacher, Freidrich. On Religion: Speeches to Its Cultured Despisers. Translated and edited by Richard Crouter. Cambridge: Cambridge University Press, 1996.

2014).[14]

Until thirty years ago, the Alevi faith was taught through oral tradition by religious leaders descended from the Prophet Muhammad and Imam Ali. The survival of the tradition across many years can be attributed to the discrimination that Alevis have been exposed to in their own countries (Aykan, et all, 2010; Cosan-Eke, 2021).[15] Besides the rich stories in oral history, Alevis claim a central text, called *Buyruk*, which is often cited as a primary source about Alevi beliefs and value system. The *Buyruk* contains Alevi history, rituals, morals and the stories and poems of historical prominent figures of the Alevi faith (such as Hacı Bektaş-i Veli, Pir Sultan Abdal, Hatayi etc).[16] In Alevi and Bektaschi poetry, *Buyruk* texts, and ritual texts, reference is made to the Four Gates Forty Steps doctrine.

This spiritual path to 'unlearning'—which is known in its basic form as the 'Four Gates' and was spread by other mystical directions—forms the core of the Alevi value system (Agucenoglu, 2014).[17] The four gates, namely 1. *Şeriat* ('The *Shari'ah*')[18], 2. *Tarîkat* ('The Way')[19], 3. *Marîfet* ('The Knowledge') and 4. *Hakîkat* ('The Truth'), which an Alevi must pass through to reach God and achieve human perfection—called *"Insan-i Kamil"* in Alevism—consist of ten structured stages/steps each.

The first gate *"Seriat"* (order) stands for the acquisition of the basic knowledge of the Alevi faith to reach the perfect human being (*Insan-i Kamil*). It is the gate through which one learns self-control based on physical needs, behaviors, and ambitions.[20] An Alevi needs a guide or a

---

[14] Sözer. Hande. 2014. "Managing Invisibility: Dissimulation and Identity Maintenance among Alevi Bulgarian Turks". Brill: *Balkan Studies Library Series*. pp: 178–200.

[15] Erdemir Aykan, Cahit Korkmaz, Halil Karaçalı, Muharrem Erdem, Theresa Weitzhofer, Umut Beşpınar. 2010. *Alevilerin Bakışaçısı ile Türkiye'de Ayrımcılık*. Ankara: Dipnot Bas. Yay. Ltd. Şti.

[16] Karolewski, Janina.2018." Discovering Alevi Rituals by Analysing Manuscripts: Buyruk Texts and Individual Notebooks". Johannes Zimmermann, Janina Karolewski, Robert Langer (eds). *Transmission Processes of Religious Knowledge and Ritual Practice in Alevism between Innovation and Reconstruction*. Berlin: Peter Lang.

[17] Agucenoglu, Hüseyin. 2014. „Ethik im Alevitentum". In: Hamid Reza Yousefi / Harald Seubert (Hrsg.): Ethik im Weltkontext. Geschichten – Erscheinungsformen – Neuere Konzepte. Wiesbaden: Springer Verlag, pp: 149-158

[18] When Alevis use the term Sharia, they do not mean the Islamic legal system "Sharia" as religious law. It is only the prerequisite for observing the rules of the religion, which is perceived, understood and learned by seeing, hearing and participating. Or the legal system represents the acquisition of basic knowledge of the Alevi faith.

[19] The second gate *"tarikat"* is reaching by making a promise (acknowledge) to the Alevi community. The term sect is used in Turkish for a group with a certain religious tradition, but this term is not the same meaning as in this gate, the purpose of this gate is to understand and realize the meaning of belief of the people individually.

[20] The basic pillar of Alevi faith is united in this one phrase. "Control your hand, your loin and your tongue- auf türkisch: *eline, beline, diline, sahip ol*". Control your hands: It stands for "good deeds", so: don't

master (leader) as a companion to acquire this basic knowledge about Alevism. This system, which includes every *dede/ana* (clergy) named in the faith and the *talip* (student or follower), is called the hearth system that means family and descent. In the *ocak* system, every family among the Alevis is dependent on a *Pir* or *Mürshid* family descended from the Prophet and Imam Ali. Therefore, Alevi religious leaders have a saint status that is passed down from father to son.

The second gate, "*Tarikat*" (mystical path), can be entered with the promise (*ikrar*) of the person to have a life as required by faith. The purpose of this door is to understand and recognize the importance of faith and collective unity. This is the process by which one finds their place in the community and always tries to align their actions with the consensus in the community. In this door, the person must be mature to evaluate or criticize themselves. Then, he/she should have a consensus with the community he/she belongs to. Finally, the community to which he/she belongs should have a consensus to accept this person into the community.

This is followed by the gate of knowledge (*Marifet*), through which one realizes the difference between the external (*zahiri*) and the hidden (*batini*) knowledge; it represents the mystical knowledge of God and is the prerequisite for desired perfection. At this door, body, emotion, mind, and spirit unite or try to achieve unity and understanding. This understanding guides people on the path of worship and religious rituals. The main Alevi religious ritual that is called *cem erkanı*,[21] realizes this commitment. Those who go through this door deepen the teaching and meaning of the scholars, and this door prepares people for the fourth and final gate (truth).

The fourth and final gate in the perfection of human being is called *Hakikat* (truth), which represents the highest attainable rank. At the center of the Alevi faith is humanity as a being who seeks itself and wants to know itself. Only man can experience himself as a whole and recognize himself, therefore man understands himself not only in the mind, but also

---

steal, don't do anything wrong...don't take anything you didn't put there yourself. Control your loin: It represents strong personality, so: have backbone, don't stoop to injustice...sexual contact with more than one person taboo invoking this commandment. Control your tongue: That is: do not lie, do not lead anyone into temptation, into error...do not say anything that you have not seen yourself. The prohibition of killing, theft, slander, and adultery apply to Alevis towards all people. In this way, they want to promote humanity in the world.

[21] Die Cem-Zeremonie – Gottesdienst der Aleviten – Alevitische Gemeinde Duisburg e.V. (alevi-du.com) (retrieved on 22.06.2021)

in the conscious harmony of feeling and body. At this gate, it is understood that truth (truthfulness) in this wholeness is the key to self-knowledge. At this stage, man, who has overcome his ego, has already left self-knowledge behind; understand the truth and the person is on the way to God. This gate reveals the experience of divinity and the cycle to perfection by spiritual evolution of the human being (*Insān al-Kāmil*). In Alevi faith, this cycle (i.e *Devriye*) embraces two sides of creation: one from spirituality to plurality, another from plurality to the spirituality.[22]

Explaining Alevism within Alevi theology requires a deep mystical analysis because its theology encompasses many subjects, like rituals, divine beings, the history of religions, and the concept of religious truth. As I mentioned earlier, the general tendency among definitions of Alevism is that not enough effort is made to specify the Alevi faith within its own value system. Alevism is mostly discussed in terms of political regulations, economic opportunities, and legal procedures that are necessary for the life of the faith and the realization of its rituals. For this reason, Alevism is used more as a political than theological concept.

Migration of Alevis to Europe

Alevi migration to Europe can be traced back to the 1960s due to high population growth, widespread unemployment, slow economic growth (especially in rural areas), and the increase in political pressures against Alevis in Turkey. Some scholars who have focused on Turkish labour migration to Germany have argued that the tendency of Alevis to migrate is stronger than that of Turkish Sunnis (Faist 2000; Martin 1991).[23] Alevis did not live as a separate group from the general Turkish immigrant groups there for a long time (Cosan Eke, 2014).[24]

In the early 1990s, Alevism began to be discussed more frequently in the public sphere, in Turkish state policy, and in the diaspora due to increasing social and political mobility processes that were based in ethnic and religious identities (Yavuz, 2003[25]; Sökefeld, 2008[26]; Solms-Baruth,

---

[22] Aytac, Pakize. 2011. "Icimizdeki Kainat – The Universe inside us". *Alevilik Araştırmaları Dergisi Sayı* 1 - Yaz 2011 https://issuu.com/guraysatici/docs/sayi1 (retrived on 25.06.2021)

[23] Faist, Thomas. 2000. The Volume and Dynamics of International Migration and Transnational Social Spaces, Oxford University Press, Oxford. Martin, Philip L.1991. The Unfinished Story: Turkish Labour Migration to Western Europe, Geneva: International Labour Office.

[24] Cosan Eke Deniz. 2014. "Transnational Communities: Alevi Immigrants in Europa". *Journal of Alevism-Bektashism Studies* . 2014;(10):167 - 194.

[25] Yavuz, M. Hakan. 2003. Islamic Political Identities in Turkey. Oxford: Oxford University Press.

[26] Sökefeld, Martin. 2008. Struggle of Recognition: The Alevi Movement in Germany and in Transnational Space. Berghahn Books.

2011).[27] But the turning point for the Alevi movement was the Sivas massacre in Turkey on July 2, 1993. Thirty-seven people (thirty-three of Alevi origin) were burned to death when an Islamist extremist group set fire to a hotel in Sivas. Later, on March 12, 1995, another person fired shots at an Alevi coffee house in Gaziosmanpaşa, a poor neighborhood in Istanbul inhabited mainly by Alevis. Following this attack, Alevi demonstrations broke out across the country. Twenty Alevis were killed during these protests, including a Dede (Alevi religious leader). Due to the increasing pressure and violence against Alevis in Turkey, especially after the 1993 Sivas massacre and the Gazi incident in 1995, sharpened the boundaries between Sunnis and Alevis. Until the late 1980s, Alevis were predominantly portrayed as part of leftist groups. Their political identity was seen as more prominent than their religious beliefs among both Alevis and non-Alevis. Since the 1990s, the religious dimension of the Alevi identity has started to come to the fore and Alevi organizations have accelerated their struggle for their right to be recognized as a separate religious community from Sunni Muslims. The German-based AABF (Federation of Alevi Communities in Germany, Almanya Alevi Birlikleri Federasyonu) plays a significant role in this process.

The AABF was established in 1989. It is the most effective organization in Europe with about 700,000 members and the 160-member organizations throughout Germany.[28] The AABF that has the largest Alevi memberships abroad has reached enough power to be able to determine the strategies of Alevi movement during the recognition process of the Alevi community not only Germany but also many European countries. The Alevi Community of Germany is a recognized religious community under Article 7 (3) of the Basic Law and represents the interests of its members as an appointed member of the German Islam Conference and the Integration Summit of the Federal Government.[29] One of the most important achievements of the Alevi community in Germany is the introduction of Alevi religious education in eight German states (Aksünger, 2013[30]; Eißler, 2017[31]; Sökefeld,

---

[27]Solms- Baruth, Carolina. 2011. The Making and Unmaking of Ethnic Boundaries: the Alevis in Germany. Budapest: Central European University, Nationalism Studies Programm.

[28] Home - Alevitische Gemeinde Deutschland e.V.

[29] Basic Law for the Federal Republic of Germany - Article 7 (3): Religious education shall be an ordinary subject in public schools, with the exception of non-denominational schools. Notwithstanding the state's right of supervision, religious instruction shall be given in accordance with the principles of the religious communities. No teacher may be obliged to teach religious education against his or her will.

[30]Aksünger, Handan. 2013.*Jenseits des Schweigegebots. Alevitische Migrantenselbstorganisationen und zivilgesellschaftliche Integration in Deutschland und den Niederlanden.* Münster: Waxmann Verlag.

[31] Eißler, Friedmann (Hrsg.). 2017. *Aleviten in Deutschland. Grundlagen, Veränderungsprozesse, Perspektiven,*

2015).[32]

After the establishment of AABF in Germany in 1990, Holland Alevi-Bektasi Social and Cultural Centres Federation (HAKDER) was founded.[33] Since 2015, the principle that Alevism maintains a unique and independent belief from Islam has been included in the constitution to prevent the attempts of the Islamic groups' pressure. There are nearly 100,000 Alevis living in Holland and 10 Alevi-Bektasi Cultural Centres in different cities of there.[34]

The British Alevi Federation (BAF), which was established in 1993, is the umbrella organization in Great Britain which is formed by the unity of Scotland, Wales and Northern Ireland. Nearly 500 thousand Alevi's live in the UK and there are 18 Alevi cultural centres and *cemevis*.[35] The National Education Curriculum Committee has agreed to have Alevism taught at primary and secondary schools in the UK. But Alevi religious education in the UK schools is conducted at the local level rather than at national or federal states level (Jenkins & Cetin, 2017).[36] Many Alevis living in the UK wrote the "Alevi" option in the religion field of their 2021 Census forms so as to be more visible and have equal opportunities.[37] In Switzerland, where 70,000 Alevis live and which has a federal structure with 26 cantons, Alevism is defined as a religion independent from Islam (Beyeler and Suter Reich, 2008).[38] The teaching of Alevism has been included in the Zurich curriculum, while other religions (Christianity, Judaism, and Islam) are taught in school. The Swiss Alevi Federation was founded in 1998 and includes 12 Alevi organizations throughout the country. The migration of Alevis to France began in the 1970s. The number of Alevis is estimated to be between 120,000 and 150,000 out of 450,000 Turks in France.[39] The French Federation of Alevis (FUAF), founded in 1998, coordinates the activities

EZW-Texte 211, 3., überarbeitete Auflage, Berlin.
[32] Sökefeld, Martin. 2015. *Aleviten in Deutschland.* Identitätsprozesse einer Religionsgemeinschaft in der Diaspora. Biefeld: transcript Verlag.
[33] Over ons – HAKDER (23.06.2021)
[34] "Alevi Union Europe". 2015. European Parliement, Brussels/Belgium. 18.03.2015.
[35] Erbil calling for Alevism to be recognised in 2021 Census - Londra Gazete (retrieved on 23.06.2021)
[36] Jenkins, Celia & Cetin, Ümit. 2017. "From a 'sort of Muslim' to 'proud to be Alevi': the Alevi religion and identity project combatting the negative identity among second generation Alevis in the UK". National Identities.
[37] AleviNet | Britanya Alevi Federasyonu | Cemevi (retrieved on 23.06.2021)
[38] Beyeler, Sarah and Virginia Suter Reich.2008. "Inkorporation von zugewanderten Religionsgemeinschaften in der Schweiz am Beispiel der Aleviten und der Ahmadiyya". Schweizerische Zeitschrift für Religion und Kulturgeschichte, vol.102, pp.233-259 (243).
[39] Anne Blanchard-Laizé, Anne. 2018 "Un centre culturel pour les Turques Alevis". Ouest-France, 29 September 2018. < Un centre culturel pour les Turques Alevis (ouest-france.fr)>. (retrieved on 23.06.2021).

of its member associations at the national level (Kosulu, 2013)[40] and has 37 Alevi cultural centres and 20,000 active members (EU, 2015).[41] In France, Alevism is not lived as a faith but as a culture and is described with the principles of secularism, tolerance and humanism. The first Alevi cultural center in Denmark was founded in Arhus as Haci Bektasi Veli Cultural Centre in 1994 after the Sivas Massacre. In 1999, the Unity of Denmark Alevi Federation was established with the founding of six Alevi cultural centres throughout the country. Alevism in Denmark have been formally recognized as a faith and has received formalized status wherein Alevis have the same rights as Christians in Denmark.[42] The first Sweden Alevi Cultural Center was founded in 1995 after Gazi events in Istanbul. Alevism has been recognized as a unique and individual religion in Sweden since 2012. Alevis living in Sweden are estimated 12,000 and the Sweden Alevi Federation has in the region of 3,000 memberships and six Alevi Associations throughout the country.[43] In Belgium, the first Alevi organization was established in 1994. More than 10 Alevi associations came together under the Federation of Alevi Associations in Belgium (BABF) by 2008. BABF is defined itself as a lay and democratic organization[44]:

Beyond the above named national Alevi Federations in Austria, Germany, France, Belgium, Denmark, Netherlands, Switzerland, Norway, England and Sweden, there are Alevi Associations in the different cities of Italy, Romania, Norway and Cyprus. The Alevi associations and Federations in these European countries joined together to form the European Confederation of Alevi Communities (AABK) in 2002. Today, there are on average more than 270 Alevi associations belonging to AABK across Europe. Estimates of the number of Alevis living in Europe are generally debated, but the Confederation of the European Alevi Community claims that this number is around 1.5 million (Aksünger-Kizil & Kahraman, 2018: 137).[45] Today, the Alevis and Alevism have become more visible thanks to the accessibility of mass media and the establishment of Alevi associations that empower the

[40] Kosulu, Deniz. 2013. "The Alevi Quest in Europe through the Redefinition of the Alevi Movement: Recognition and Political Participation, A Case Study of the FUAF in France". In Jorgen S. Nielsen (ed). Muslim Political Participation in Europe. Edinburg University Press

[41] "Alevi Union Europe". 2015. European Parliement, Brussels/Belgium. 18.03.2015

[42] "Alevi Union Europe". 2015. European Parliement, Brussels/Belgium. 18.03.2015

[43] "Alevi Union Europe". 2015. European Parliement, Brussels/Belgium. 18.03.2015

[44] <http://www.ejustice.just.fgov.be/tsv_pdf/2008/02/28/08033120.pdf > (retrived on 23.05.2021)

[45] Aksünger-Kizil, Handan &Kahraman Yilmaz. 2018. Das anatolische Alevitentum Geschichte und Gegenwart einer in Deutschland anerkannten Religionsgemeinschaf. Hamburg: Landeszentrale für politische Bildung, Hamburg

transnational networks among Alevis.

In recent years, both Alevism, as a political and theological concept, and the Alevi movement, which has transformed as a diaspora movement, have increased in importance on the agendas of European countries. This is due in part to Alevism being discussed as exemplary for the possibilities of religious and political pluralism and integration in Western Europe (Cosan Eke, 2021[46]; Massicard, 2006[47]; Deutsche Welle, February 9th, 2011[48], Ulram, 2009[49]).

Having presented the general framework of the religious and socio-political situation of the Alevi community in European countries in the context of their organizations and the transnational networks they have built, we can elaborate on the discussion of the main research topic chosen in this section: Alevis in Austria will be analyzed in order to shed light on the impact of representation on religious groups. To obtain information about the representation of Alevis and their organizational processes in Austria, let us now look at the situation of religious groups in this country.

Religious Groups in Austria

Austria is based on the principle of equal treatment of all legally recognized religious communities in terms of their rights and resources and defines itself as having an inclusive model (Mattes & Rosenberger, 2015).[50] However, the legal process for granting citizenship is challenging, with high expectation for integration, and represents an exclusionary model.

The legal-historical context is important to explain if one is to understand the situation of Alevis in Austria, since the contradiction between the exclusionary citizenship model and the inclusive religious administration model in Austria affects the organization of Alevis. The increasing right-wing populist approach in the country means that Alevis

[46] Coşan Eke, Deniz. 2021. *"The Changing Leadership Roles of Dedes in the Alevi Movement .Ethnographic Studies on Alevi Associations in Turkey and Germany from the 1990s to the Present"*. Bielefeld: Transcript.
[47] Massicard, Elise.2006. "Alevist Mobilization in Germany and the Perspective of Turkish Integration in the EU". *International interdisciplinary workshop 'Ethnic mobilization in the New Europe'*. Brussels, 21-22/04/2006.
[48] Deutsche Welle, 09.02.2011: "Almanya´da Aleviler Uyuma Örnek" (Alevis in Germany is an example for Integration) <http://www.dw.com/tr/almanyada-aleviler-uyuma-%C3%B6rnek/a-14829865> (retrieved on 16.06.2021).
[49] Ulram. Peter. A. 2009. Integration in Österreich. Einstellungen, Orientierungen, und Erfahrungen von Migrantinnen und Angehörigen der Mehrheitsbevölkerung. Wien. GfK-Austria GmbH.
[50] Mattes & Rosenberger. 2015. Islam and Muslims in Austria. In M. Burchardt & I. Michalowski (eds). After Integration, Islam and Politik. Springer.

must deal with various prejudices both as a Turkish immigrant group and as a belief group included with Islamic law. In the 1950s, 89% of the Austrian population was identified as Catholic, with 6.2% being Protestant and 3.8% being non-denominational (Mattes and Rosenberger 2015: 130). However, because of the effects of World War II, the beginning of the 1960s saw a demand for labor. For this reason, and similar to other post-War European nations, many migrants came to Austria through the 1964 labor agreement called the Austria Recruitment Agreement. Firstly, liken Turkish immigrants in Germany, Alevi immigrants in Austria defined their position in the country as many guest workers did. However, political, and economic instability in Turkey influenced the plans of Alevi immigrants in Austria and they decided to bring their families from Turkey (Hahn & Stöger, 2014).[51] According to the Migration Policy Institute, "In 1969, the number of foreign workers from Turkey and Yugoslavia stood at 76,500 but by 1973, numbers had almost tripled to 227,000 - 178,000 of whom came from Yugoslavia and 27,000 from Turkey"(Jandl & Kraler, 2003).[52]

The number of Muslims living in Austria increased from 0.3 in the 1971 census to 2% in the 1991 census and to 4.2% in the 2001 census, when about 350,000 people reported Islam as their religious belief. After almost fifteen years, there are still no official statistics on Muslims, but according to the Austrian Integration Fund (ÖIF), about 8% (700,000) of the population were Muslims.[53] It is estimated that of theMuslims living in Austria, 85% are Sunnis, 12% Shiites, 3% Alevis, Ahmadis and other Islamic groups. In addition, Turks constituted the largest group among Muslims living in Austria in 2009 with 109,000 or 21% of Muslims (Sezgin, 2019).[54] At the beginning of 2021, there were about 118,000 Turkish citizens living in Austria with Turks representing the fourth largest group of foreigners (Statista, 2021).[55] As mentioned above, statistical information on Muslims and Alevis is insufficient. It is claimed that Alevis did not want to organize any cultural associations for Alevis until the 1980s (Aksünger-Kizil, 2018:175).[56] They lived and were

---

[51] Hahn, Sylvia & Stöger, Georg. 2014. „50 Jahre österreichisch-türkisches Anwerbeabkommen". Salzburg: Fachbereich Geschichte/Zentrum für Ethik und Armutsforschung – Univ. Salzburg.
[52] Article: Austria: A Country of Immigration? | migrationpolicy.org
[53] Islam europäischer Prägung: Österreichischer Integrationsfonds ÖIF (retrieved on 25.06.2021)
[54] Sezgin, Zeynep. 2019. „Islam and Muslim Minorotoes in Austria: Historical Context and Current Challenges of Integration. Journal of International Migration and Integration. 20: 869-889.
[55] Österreich - Türken 2021 | Statista (retrieved on 29.06.2021)

[56] Aksünger-Kizil H. Zur Situation der anatolischen Aleviten in Deutschland und Österreich. in Islam Europäischer Prägung. 2018. S. 161-181

accepted primarily as Turkish or Muslim.

Alevi Migration in Austria

Alevis have been living in Austria for almost six decades—since the beginning of labor migration from Turkey—but have been recognized publicly since the 2000s. As mentioned above, statistical information on Alevis in Austria is insufficient and often debated. It is claimed that 10-20% of Austrian Muslims were Alevi (Öktem, 2015)[57]. According to the Austrian Federal Chancellery, the number of Alevis in Austria has been estimated at 70,000–80,000 (2023:53)[58].

In Austria, religion and state relations are characterized according to a shared cooperation model. Religious communities can decide their religious arrangements but are recognized by the state and granted certain legal and financial privileges, such as state subsidies. Since 1912, Islam, including Alevism, has been recognized with the status of a statutory body called Islam law[59]. In 1979, the Islamic Religious Community in Austria (Islamische Glaubensgemeinschaft in Österreich-IGGiÖ) was accepted as the official representative for all Muslims in the country. Accordingly, Muslims in Austria gained the same rights as other legally recognized religious communities (i.e. Protestant, Catholic, and Jewish) (Sezgin, 2019)[60].

After the collapse of the Habsburg monarchy at the end of the First World War, the Muslim population of Austria was reduced to a few hundred (Kern 2015, 60 Sezgin, 2019)[61]. However, the Muslim population in this country has started to increase again due to guest worker immigrants since the 1960s. For this reason, it is not possible to talk about a Muslim organization in Austria before 1979. In the same year, in 1979, the Islamic Faith Community gained the status of a privileged corporation of public law (Körperschaft des öffentlichen Rechts)[62]. Each religious group has one legal

[57] Öktem, Kerem (2015). "Austria". In Scharbrodt, Oliver; Akgönül, Samim; Alibašić, Ahmet; Nielsen, Jørgen; Racius, Egdunas (eds.). *Yearbook of Muslims in Europe, Volume 7*. Brill.
[58] Bundeskanzleramt. 2023. Religion in Austria: Overview of the religious societies recognised in Austria. Vienna.
[59] In 1912, Islam was recognized officially as a religious community with equal rights in the time of the Habsburg monarchy. The Islam Law of 1912 expressly referred to the Moslem members of the Hanafi group. The Hanafis are the largest group within Sunni Islam, accounting for over 40% of Muslims. In 1988, the Islam Law was extended to all versions of Islam and defined rights and obligations for the Islamic Religious Societies. When the recruitment of foreign laborers in the 1960s continued to increase the number of Muslims in Austria, the Islamic Community in Austria demanded new legal regulations, and the "new" Islam Law was enacted in 2015. (The Austrian Islam Law - Federal Chancellery (bundeskanzleramt.gv.at)
[60] Sezgin, Zeynep. 2019. "Islam and Muslim Minorities in Austria: Historical Context and Current Challenges of Integration". Journal of International Migration and Integration. 20:869-886.
[61] Kern, S. (2015) 'Austria's Islamic Reforms,' The New York Times, http://www.nytimes.com/2015/04/08/opinion/austrias-islamic-reforms.html?_r=0 (20.06.2021).
[62] As far as the legal status of religious communities is concerned, there are two forms in Austria: legally

status for all different groups in the same religion. Therefore, some groups in Islam such as Shiites and Alevis were troubled with the Sunni domination in the Islamic Faith Community in Austria. The Alevi Culture Society Association in St. Pölten, established in 1989, was the first Austrian Alevi Organization to protect the Alevi teaching and identity of Alevis who migrated from Turkey and to pass attendant rights on to future generations. A year later, in 1990, the Vienna association d. Alevi Ehlibeyt and Bektashi members (later the VAKB Cultural Association of Alevis in Vienna) were founded. As in the other European countries, Alevi organizations in Austria increased in Austria after the Sivas massacre in 1993 and the Gazi events in 1995. This was followed by the formation of associations in other federal states.

In 1998, the Austrian Alevi Congregations Federation (AABF) was established as the umbrella organization, that is the "Federation of Alevi Communities in Austria" (Föderation der Aleviten Österreichs-AABF). This umbrella organization now has 10 local associations and almost 6,000 members (Aksunger, Kızıl, 2017: 175). In Austria, AABF, unlike other national Alevi federations in European countries affiliated with AABK (European Alevi Bektashi Confederation), did not become an official representative body deciding on regulations regarding Alevis until 2022. The reason for this is that some of the AABF´s members left the AABF, because of their different interpretations of Alevism and they founded a new organization, called "Islamic Alevi Religious Community in Austria (IAGÖ)", in Vienna in 2009 (Eberwein, 2019:21)[63]. The Austrian Alevi Communities Federation (AABF) started negotiations with the Office of Culture in 2007, but the new members of IAGÖ applied to this office two weeks before AABF.

IAGÖ applied firstly the Federal Ministry for Education, Art, and Culture to be recognized as a different group from the Islamic Faith Community in Austria, they could not attain the right to represent the Alevis in Austria. Their application was initially rejected on the grounds that the Islamic Faith Community in Austria was already a legally recognized representative organization for Alevis in Austria and that a second Alevi group was not permitted. After only one year, this reasoning was overturned in 2010 after it was deemed unconstitutional by the Austrian Constitutional

recognized churches and religious societies and state-registered religious denominations. The denominational communities have legal personality but are not public corporations. Legal recognition by the state, on the other hand, grants a religious community the status of a corporation under public law (Körperschaft des öffentlichen Rechts), which goes hand in hand with the performance of tasks in the public interest, e.g., the right to provide religious education in all schools. (Allgemeine Informationen zu Religionen in Österreich (oesterreich.gv.at), retrieved on 29.08.2023)
[63] Microsoft Word - 20.05.2019 Das neue Islamgesetz 2015 - eine juristische Bewertung.docx (jku.at)

Court, which had approved the application by the Office of Culture. The IAGÖ was registered as a confessional community in 2010 and attained the status of a recognized religious community within the Islam Act in 2013[64]. Although the Islam Law states that the choice of name of a newly recognized denomination must be made in such a way that it may in no way cause a "risk of confusion" with already existing institutions (the AABF has existed in Austria since 1998), the IAGÖ changed its name to ALEVI in 2015 with the amendment of the Islam Law[65].

ALEVI was recognized as the official representative organization of the Alevi community in 2013[66]. As such, it is now the only legal and legitimate Alevi religious representative for all state school councils, district school councils, and all public and private schools in matters of education. As this right is legally only granted to a representative of a religious community in Austria, AABF's application remains unconfirmed. Thanks to the official state-sanctioned status of ALEVI, Alevis have gained many rights to teach their faith and rituals in Austria. For example, cemevis are recognized as places of Alevi worship in Austria. At the same time, this status provides the right to write "Alevi" and "Alevi religious education" (ARU) in the religious section of national identity cards. The Education Office of the Alevi Faith Community in Austria organizes, manages, and is responsible for the direct supervision of Alevi religious education in public and private schools. Austria offers the most opportunities to learn Alevism in schools across Europe, and there were 51 teachers and 2,028 27 students in the 2016/2017 school year. At the end of this legal status of ALEVI, a training course for teachers who teach Alevism at the schools is currently being offered at the Katkolische Pädagogische Hochschule in Vienna. Furthermore, the Chair for Alevi Theology Studies was established at the University of Vienna in September 2018. Based on the amended Islam Act 2015, Alevi Theology Studies aims primarily to promote the academic training of Alevi theologians and teachers of religion in a pluralistic Austria. Ultimately, it can be claimed that it fosters the identity formation of Alevi pupils in an integrative way and as part of Austrian society.

AABF applied to the Federal Ministry of Education, Arts and Culture, too but their application was initially rejected. Because the IAGÖ, was already a legally recognized representative organization for Alevis in Austria, and a second Alevi group was not permitted because Islamic law did not

---

[64] Gesetzlich anerkannte Kirchen und Religionsgesellschaften (oesterreich.gv.at) (retrieved on 23.06.2023)

[65] Geschichte und Gründung – ALEVI – Alevitische Glaubensgemeinschaft in Österreich (aleviten.at)

[66] "Anerkennung der Anhänger der Islamischen Alevitischen Glaubensgemeinschaft als Religionsgesellschaft" (in German). Legal Information System of the Republic of Austria. 2013. Retrieved: 2023-09-12.

provide for multiple religious communities (Religion Report, the Austrian Federal Chancellery, 2023:53). At the end of the long legal process of AABF's application, since 13 April 2022, the AABF has also been a state-recognized religious community in Austria, too. AABF changed its name to Frei Alevis (Frei Aleviten) and they have demonstrated that they have a different theology from the ALEVi group in 2022. Apart from these two Alevi communities, the Old-Alevi Community in Austria (Alt alevitischen Glaubengemeinschaft in Österreich) has been recognized as a confessional community by the Office for Religious Affairs in the Federal Chancellery (2021 Report on International Religious Freedom: Austria).

This separation of free Alevis in Austria (Frei Aleviten Österreich), Old-Alevi Community and ALEVI in the Alevi organizations of Austria is related to differences in the interpretation of Alevism as well as distinct political relations, ideological perspectives, and understandings of identity negotiation among Alevi migrants. Free Alevis defines Alevis belief as distinct from Islam, while ALEVİ emphasizes Alevis belief in relationship to Islam. As a member of the European Alevi Confederation, Free Alevis can communicate with Alevis in a wider geography through transnational networks. However, ALEVI has a more limited international network than Frei Alevis because free Alevis has a good connection with the European Alevi Confederation. ALEVI as a recognized community "has 17,351 registered members according to the figures of the relevant Minister of Education, Arts, and Culture...," (Mattes & Rosernberger, 2015: 131). It is estimated that there are approximately 6,000 members of the Frei Alevis. Based on these data, it can be possible to argue that these figures cannot reflect the representation of the most of Alevi population in the country, which has reached 70,000- 80,000.

Conclusion

This chapter showcases the importance of religious representation, which plays a central role in the transmission of religious knowledge and traditions from generation to generation. Alevi associations, which emerged as a political group after the 1990s and continue to struggle to be defined as a religious community in Europe today, are defined as the representatives of Alevis. This definition contributes not only to the basis of legal procedures in the EU constitutional order, but also to discussions of religious diversity and pluralism.

As was explained regarding the Alevi communities in Austria, Alevi organizations attempt to establish the relationship between politics and theology while representing Alevis. The diversity that exists in Alevism, especially within the Alevi Associations, is often reflected as a threat to the preservation and survival of the faith. However, thanks to the diversity of the Alevi faith, which has existed for centuries, it has very positive effects on the creation of a common society with different beliefs and cultures and the integration of Alevis wherever they live. The fact that non-Alevis present diversity in Alevism as a problem aims to manage the Alevi belief by putting it into a uniform pattern. However, the negative treatment of this diversity by the believers negatively affects the Alevi faith's limited use of its teachings, economic and political opportunities, and most importantly, the teaching of faith as a religion of love and tolerance.

Presently, Alevism has begun to take shape as a political and theological concept within a pluralistic approach that includes political theology. When including Alevism in the discussion area of political theology, we can take a brief look at the theoretical debate on the representation of religious groups to deepen this new discussion. Liberal thought and the concept of secularization cause the discussion about the distinction between public and private sphere and religion has been defined in the private sphere. However, recently, this distinction has always been increasingly criticized because it has been clearly seen that it is not possible to define a religion only in the private sphere. Furthermore, the recent increase in the effectiveness of religion in politics and in the public sphere has led to an increase in political theology debates that discuss secularization and the relationship between politics and religion. According to Laborde, political theology is "a fundamental critique of secular liberal political theory" (2014: 689).[67] Because what Laborde claims here, as Schmitt (2002) states, is that the terms belonging to the state are shaped by the secularization of the terms of the religious system.[68]

Also, Mulier argues that in self-defining collectives, representation plays a constitutive role in setting boundaries and defining a group (Mulier, 2018:508).[69] Since the legitimacy of persons and institutions with the right to represent does not include those who do not support these institutions and individuals, ignoring these persons who do not have the

[67] Laborde, C. (2014). "Three Theses About Political Theology: Some Comments on Seyla Benhabib's 'Return of Political Theology'". Critical Review of International Social and Political Philosophy, 17(6), 689-696.
[68] Schmitt, Carl, Siyasi İlahiyat, çev. Emre Zeybekoğlu, Dost Kitapevi, Ankara, 2002, s.10.
[69] Mulieri, Alessandro. 2018. "Representation as a political-theological concept: A critique of Carl Schmitt". Philosophy and Social Criticism 2018, Vol. 44(5) 507–527

right to represent is an attitude sometimes taken consciously and sometimes unconsciously. In this sense, representation can transform its legal and discursive position into a power relationship between those who have the right to represent and those who do not. This can cause the representative to change from a decision maker to an actor who determines relationships and conflicts between people. According to Mulier,

> "The idea that there is no opposition between representation and participation, but that representation is the very condition that makes it possible for political subjects to participate to democratic politics is, in essence, already present in the logic of representation as a political theological concept" (2018: 509).

In summary, being a representative of a faith first requires building a structuring model based on theology. Diversities within each belief may not form separate groups. However, Alevism has been subjected to intense pressure from political debates due to its unique processes in its own history, so they have separated into different groups. Especially after 1990, the rapidly increasing the number of the Alevi organizations made this diversity visible.

A religious pluralism perspective is needed to move this diversity within the Alevi faith from a constantly problematic area to a more conciliatory and active communication area. Pluralism, which is formed between religious groups and within a belief, provides the ground to communicate and establish relationships in a two-way relationship that creates a common society which includes said diversity by accounting for each other's differences. Indeed, as stated in the Harvard University Pluralism Project, "Pluralism is an achievement, not a predetermined outcome."

THE ROLE OF INTERRELIGIOUS DIALOGUE AND OUTREACH IN BUILDING TRUST AND STRENGTHENING SOCIAL INCLUSION IN EUROPE: THE CASE OF NETWORK FOR DIALOGUE

Amjad Saleem[1] and Aleksandra Djuric Milovanovic[2]

Introduction

Since 2015, migration to Europe has created challenges for community relations in terms of dealing with cohesive integration and a recognition of the growing diversity within communities. In recent years, European policymakers have perceived the arrival of refugees and migrants as a challenge especially as they try to address cross cutting issues of social cohesion, economy and health. Representations of the 'migrant crisis' reinforce negative perceptions of migration dynamics[3]. One narrative, which paints the notion of the arrival of refugees and migrants since 2015 as a constant flow of people that suddenly and unexpectedly pushed at the continent's Mediterranean borders, distorts the lived experience of migration and trivialise migration-related challenges. Focus on the frequency and scale of the migration undermines nuanced understanding of the causes, consequences and experiences of migrants and refugees.

This narrative inevitably polarises society, particularly those from the host community. However, as Katwala and Somerville 2016 argue, the challenge is not those on either side of the spectrum of the argument regarding migration, but the 'Anxious Middle,' those who are not strongly against migration but have several concerns about the effect of migration on their society. These concerns cannot simply be dissuaded by facts, figures and moral messaging. Whilst there must be better understanding of the content and type of messaging to secure public support, appeals to empathy are considered to be effective and stories of success are equally important (Ballinger, Rutter and Katwala, 2017). In particular, empathetic appeals through programs that support a real connection between communities and create programs to build trust (Moretti and

---

[1] Advisor, Centre for Humanitarian Diplomacy Sarajevo
[2] Senior Research Associate, Institute for Balkan Studies SASA
[3] www.medmig.info/key-findings, accessed 03 January 2022

Bozon 2017) are deemed to be most successful. Enabling more positive interactions between refugees and migrants and the local host community by coming together and learning from each other as well as about each other can provide the basis for a deeper relationship. In this case local community-based organisations, such as faith-based organisations (FBOs) and inter religious bodies, are well-placed to bridge the gap between communities, to offer opportunities for volunteering that lead to increased connection and greater humanisation of migrants (Fiddian-Qasmiyeh 2011). When such connections are based on interreligious and intercultural dialogue, they foster empathy, understanding, and mutual respect (Abu-Nimer and Smith 2016). As Ballinger, Rutter and Katwala (2017) highlight, networks of faith leaders as credible local spokespeople are more effective messengers of a positive narrative to the Anxious Middle if those leaders are themselves first-hand witnesses to the situation of refugees. However, the roles of religion and dialogue, and that which faith leaders play in promoting social inclusion and migration, have not been extensively researched, especially not from a comparative perspective. There are too few empirical studies that value this unique perspective, especially in transnational contexts where, across the migration trail, networks of religious organisations can coordinate to support refugees and migrants (Mavelli and Wilson 2017).

This paper focuses on the role of faith-based organisations (FBOs) and their grassroots work with refugees and migrants in building social cohesion across Europe. It adds to empirical studies by exploring the experience of the Network for Dialogue, a European platform of organizations, including faith-based ones working with refugees and migrants, set up by the International Dialogue Centre, KAICIID in 2019. This paper will analyse the grassroots experiences of religious actors in refugee and migrant support in the past years from several European countries included in the Network, namely: Sweden, Croatia, Serbia, Greece, and Italy. The argument put forward is that whilst interreligious and intercultural dialogue tools and practices, are vital, FBOs themselves benefit from and can contribute to a peer network that supports learning, enhances interreligious dialogue, and builds trust. Thus, FBOs need to be considered as viable partners and interlocutors in discussions around migration / refugees, social inclusion, and protection. The paper concludes that faith leaders have an important role in creating spaces for dialogue and hence building trust between communities.

The Anxious Middle

In a study of public opinion about migration in the UK, Katwala and Somerville (2016) refer to the "anxious middle," not as the far right or left but as people who have concerns about migration without being openly hostile. There is no fixed definition of who comprises the 'anxious middle,' but Katwala and Somerville (2016) identify two types of persons often found at the middle ground of public debates on migration. The first is those who are anxious about job security and wages, who tend to be from a lower middle or working classes, and who live outside London. The second type is made up of those concerned about changes to the dominant culture, who are slightly wealthier, and who live near or around London. These two types represent the combined demographic that voted for Brexit; however it is often the opinion of many of the second type that strengthens polarised nationalist conversations. The latter type also contributes to conversations around migration in Europe, as they are largely sceptical about government handling of immigration and worried about the effects of immigration on society and the economy. Such persons are not necessarily hostile towards immigrants, especially those considered to be skilled workers, and may be open to changing their opinion as public opinion fluctuates. Nevertheless, this type can theoretically be swayed by information that frames migration as justifying their fears of its consequences.

While a group can be encouraged and influenced to change their opinion, it is important to note that altering narratives about migration does not start with myth busting. The concept of giving people the real facts to stem worry has been shown to fail (Ballinger, Rutter and Katwala 2017). This is largely because immigration is influenced by public policy where public trust is in short supply. Thus, there is a risk of further misinformation and of people not being convinced through information sharing. Numerous academic studies show that increased contact with migrants weakens anti-immigration sentiments among the public. In other words, there is greater worry regarding cultural or ethnic diversity and integration among people who have little personal contact with refugees and migrants. Attempts to change public opinion around refugees and migrants also need to engage with people's genuine real-world concerns by providing a space for open discussions of solutions that acknowledge genuine difficulties (Dempster and Hargrave 2017). There is need to both understand the roots of expressed fear and to tell stories that dispel stereotypes, such as those of people from the anxious middle befriending refugees or those that more broadly humanise migrants (Hamlin 2021). There is also a need to build trust between stakeholders. However, this cannot be done without also ensuring that people can engage with each other through joint activities with a common aim (British Red Cross 2019). There is, therefore, a need at the governmental level to build trust and change narrative on migration by focussing on the anxious middle who are open to receiving messages about the benefits of migration whilst acknowledging contexts, pressures and potential outcomes of practical responses (Katwala and Sommerville 2016).

Role of Dialogue - Interfaith and Intercultural

Constructive contact with those who are different requires having intercultural and interreligious competences as integral life skills. This involves overcoming fears of the Other, strengthening self-awareness and empowering internal voices. In this sense dialogue plays a role in enhancing understanding and cooperation (Abu-Nimer and Smith 2016). The narrative around outreach and engagement speaks to the importance of building empathy for refugees and migrants. (Hamlin 2021). Dialogue that promotes fruitful interactions is necessary to support peaceful coexistence in diverse societies. Dialogue processes can transform individuals in societies in a way that increases authentic social cohesion, because it strengthens trust and understanding, and enables real relationships to be built across differences. Dialogue is a two-way process of mutual accommodation that can only take place if both "sides" have a deeper understanding of the needs, perspectives, desires, fears, and priorities of the other. It is not just about understanding what the other is saying, but what they really mean. It refers to something beyond just an academic exercise, but that dialogue is part of daily life during which different groups (including cultural and religious groups) interact with each other directly, and where tensions between them are the most tangible (Andrabi 2020). In this sense it is important to look at interreligious or intercultural dialogue.

Interreligious dialogue is about people of different faiths coming to a mutual understanding and respect that allows them to live and cooperate with each other despite their differences. The term refers to cooperative and positive interaction between people of different faiths/religious traditions, at both the individual and institutional level. Each party remains true to their own beliefs while respecting the right of the other to practise their faith freely. Interfaith dialogue is not just words or talks, it includes human interaction and relationships. It is also about handling the encounters with religious difference-dialogue in daily life. Thus, adherents of differing religious traditions encounter each other in order to break down the walls of division that stand at the centre of most wars with the objective being peace (Andrabi 2020).

As the KAICIID interfaith dialogue manual (2021) states, dialogue is more than conversation. The goal is not to find a resolution to a problem or to settle on a specific action, but to explore and find common ground, leading to solutions or cooperation. This is a particularly important tool in diverse societies that seek to incorporate and use that diversity for positive outcomes. Dialogue becomes an effective approach to strengthening social cohesion within culturally and religiously diverse societies because it allows for people to maintain their various identities while still finding common ground. "Dialogue, whether interreligious or intercultural, provides valuable support for involving and building bridges between all parties, regardless of social background, religious beliefs, national borders, or political and economic interests".[4] Furthermore, "the purpose of interreligious dialogue is to convene people from different backgrounds, religions, cultures, and identities in a safe and constructive space to discover similarities and identify differences.

Interreligious dialogue rests on the same basic values as dialogue. It differs in that religious identities are central to those engaged in the process. Religious identities are crucial to creating a space for dialogue because it allows opportunities for people to speak from a particular position and to learn from each other. However, the aim of dialogue is not to change the ideas of people's religion or faith, but to find common ground between religions by focusing on communities, and through an emphasis on harmony and peace, to find solutions to common problems (Andrabi 2020). In this sense, creating a space for people from different faith backgrounds to come together provides them with an opportunity to talk with and listen to each other, getting to know and learning to understand the 'Other' and the differences that exist in identity. In interfaith dialogue the aim is to approach the Other in a spirit of tolerance, truthfulness, sincerity, love, respect, and good will, without

---

[4] https://www.kaiciid.org/publications-resources/guide-interreligious-dialogue, page 16 (accessed on 10 January 2022)

willing the other to accept their own beliefs or ideas.

It is important to build intercultural and interreligious competences in order to create global citizens and to foster peaceful and cohesive communities (Abu-Nimer and Smith 2016). Thus, intercultural and interreligious dialogue become essential tools. Faith-based organisations often use and support interreligious dialogue in their work with communities at the grassroots level. "In intercultural dialogue participants come from different backgrounds and gather to talk from their explicitly stated cultural identity lenses to create better understanding of certain challenges."[5] Dialogue helps people who are on different sides of an argument—particularly those who are marginalised and excluded—to understand that they are not alone in their hopes and fears. Nor do participants need to be afraid or ashamed to ask difficult questions in seeking understanding, only to respect and ultimately accept differences without compromising one's beliefs or identity. The purpose of interfaith dialogue is thus to increase understanding and respect for other religious systems and institutions, thereby increasing an appreciation of their values. "Dialogue should enhance our sensitivity to the feelings of all professing religious people in their relationship with God. Good dialogue should, in addition, result in the deepening of the faith of every participant" (Andrabi, 2020 266).

The aim of dialogue is to overcome misunderstandings and dispel stereotypes in order to gain deeper mutual understanding. Rather than necessarily agreeing on a point of view, dialogue is about recognising and developing mutual respect to build sustainable relationships. By focusing on common needs, dialogue builds bridges and transforms human relations. It fosters deeper understanding, so that even though disagreements may persist, an appreciation for Others' perspectives can emerge. Dialogue is a powerful tool that can be undertaken in both formal and informal settings. Dialogical approaches provide a certain code to undertake informal dialogue. This determines a set of principles to be followed in interactions with the Other. It provides for a quality of interaction that promotes a means of getting involved in different creative processes where the participants can feel included and empowered, safe to be transparent, to take risks, to be open to what others have to say, and to be able to take a long-term view of the issues at hand (KAICIID 2021).

---

[5] https://network4dialogue.eu/resources/, page 14 (accessed 01 February 2022)

These are important ways to strengthen cohesion, since it contributes to identity maintenance, whilst finding common ground. In taking a dialogical approach, misperceptions and fears can be dispelled, as understanding is built that can lay the groundwork for practical approaches to peaceful coexistence. Such a foundation is extremely important when faced with the politics of identity, as we are increasingly faced, regarding migrants, host communities and perceptions. As social beings, we have a unique collection of thoughts, habits, and beliefs that define who we are. These attributes of the self have been imprinted on our lives through a series of events and contexts. This shapes our identity and our expressions and representations of it. As Amartya Sen writes "Identity incorporates the ideas, beliefs, qualities, and expressions that make a person who he/she is. This self-perception is modelled by relation with others and with an individual's own context in time" (Sen 2007). Identities are important because they form the basis of who we believe ourselves to be and how we fit in with the world. One general collective form of identity is culture, which is socially transmitted to the individual in order to construct the group's common views and meanings. While cultures may differ from one another, one aspect they all share is that they provide a framework for fulfilling the primary human need to belong. Thus, humans strive to fulfil this basic need to belong through one or more of the broader collective identities, in addition to the recognition of their own personal identity. Their cultural identity often overlaps with language and ethnicity, and sometimes also with religion. At the same time, a religion itself may include several cultures, resulting in the two overlapping most of the time, which in turn may sometimes be the cause off several complications across the two areas.

It is important to also discuss cultures and worldviews as they are mutually reinforcing. A worldview is how one looks at the world, the sum of all beliefs, experiences, and knowledge which impacts how one views the world to a greater or lesser extent, depending upon the person and the importance of the belief to that person, their experience or knowledge (Stanley 2019). Culture on the other hand is how you describe human connection and interactions in societies and groups. Thus, whilst the worldview of each person is as unique as a fingerprint, our cultural view can be something shared between people. Often a geographical area where we live can impact our worldview and cultural understanding. Essentially this means that our worldview and our culture are two different ways of explaining how we view the world, but each is unique from the other. One's worldview affects cultural identity and our culture affects our worldview, but worldview does not define culture and culture does not define worldview. Yet once a person is embedded in these basic assumptions, it will be difficult to "believe" other orderings. However, despite deeply rooted articulations and their long-lasting nature, beliefs may change over long periods of time. This is because the ongoing interaction with other cultures and experiences within one's own culture, and personal life, constantly reshape their worldview in an uncontrollable way (Note et al 2009).

Worldviews are thus important in dialogue because they include all the conscious and unconscious elements that form and influence a person's perception of reality. A worldview can also be seen as dynamic since an individual's perception of reality may change over time. Therefore, inter-worldview dialogue aims to improve mutual understanding across different worldviews—including numerous identities and sub-identities—and it opens pathways for more inclusive language. When we feel unacknowledged or receive negative reactions or feedback to our personal identities, we tend to suppress our identity and develop coping narratives. Sometimes these narratives are used to justify violence against others and foster further exclusion. Sometimes, such narratives prompt the inclusion of only those with whom we share that particular identity. The good news is that the same is true in reverse; when identities are recognised and affirmed, we also develop narratives about them. Ultimately these stories act as a protective mechanism and directly affect how we interact with others and influence those who we choose to either engage with or avoid. Thus, when we have a single story that has been built upon negative stereotypes and false perceptions of those who are different from us, we can easily become prone towards prejudice and discrimination. Prejudice is more likely to develop and persist where groups have different or conflicting key values or are seen as intrinsically different; where identity is seen in terms of belonging to particular groups and there is emotive stereotype put forward (Abrams 2010). As Fiske (2017) writes, some stereotype content is pervasive across cultures, with variations in intensity but not patterns: Women and older people who comply with prescriptive stereotypes are cherished as warm but incompetent; those who resist are resented as competent but cold. Stereotype content across cultures suggests these gender, age, and class stereotypes plausibly serve a common adaptation to disparities in societal rank, when coupled with some degree of interdependence. Dialogue allows us to become more aware of the power dynamics of identities and hierarchy of identities. Dialogue requires clarity of purpose and also helps to build trust between communities.

What is Trust?

Trust is often seen as something warm and fuzzy but not quantifiable. Yet trust makes us feel safe and comfortable. So, whilst trust is dismissed from the professional sphere as being something intangible, from a leadership perspective it is still seen as a much-valued trait. Leaders who cannot inspire trust cannot lead; there will be no followership. Trust is the glue that ensures cohesion between diverse communities. The reason so much reluctance to professionally consider the importance of trust whilst acknowledging it as a personal trait is that trust is often seen as a leap of faith. It is based on one's worldview and experience. Likewise, trust involves taking risks because while it takes a long time to build, trust can be broken very quickly. When times call for fundamental change, trust is often hard to come by. Yet trust is essential to developing relationships with individuals. So, the message is clear: To be trusted, one must be trustworthy! Building trust is the essential foundation for building healthy communities. It inspires changes in individual lives and interpersonal relationships which in turn can catalyse social action and legislative change (Corcoran 2010). Building trust must begin from the personal level as the most needed reforms in our communities require levels of political courage and trust-based collaboration that can only be achieved by individuals who have the vision, integrity, and persistence to call out the best in others and sustain deep and long-term outcomes. Without trust, authentic collaboration is unattainable. From history, the likes of Mandela, Ghandi, and King worked off social capital based on trust. Trust is also a matter of life and death. If people don't trust others in the community, this can lead to violent conflict and with that cause the death of innocents or the infringement on individual rights. So, without trust there cannot be real reform to address the social challenges. Thus, trust has to emerge across social and racial divides from the bottom up. The honest conversation must first build the bridge across communal divides.

In this light, it is worth exploring the 'Trust Quotient' which has been developed as an online self-assessment tool to measure an individual's ability to garner 'Trust' (Maister, Galford and Green 2000). Whilst the tool is itself useful, what is more useful to consider are the attributes behind the 'Trust Quotient': credibility, reliability, intimacy, and self-orientation. The equation identified below is thought provoking as it makes the concept of trust more practical and posits the notion that the idea of trust is very much linked to the individual and dependent on the level of one's self-orientation.

$$Trustworthiness \ = \frac{Crediblility + Reliability + Intimacy}{Self - Orientation}$$

The Trust Quotient has one variable in the denominator and three in the numerator. The three numerator variables improve trustworthiness while the denominator can reduce trustworthiness.

Increasing the value of the factors in the numerator increases the value of trust. Increasing the value of the denominator (self-orientation) decreases the value of trust. The Trust Quotient provides a scientific, analytical, and actionable framework for helping organizations and individuals improve their businesses and lives. Thus, trust is a consequence of good behaviour, not an ingredient, and while it takes decades to build it can vanish overnight based on the ego and self-orientation

Exploring the attributes of the Trust Quotient in more detail, we see that:

Credibility is about rating "what you say and how believable you are to others." In other words, one must be and sound credible if they are asking others to follow their lead. Credibility also comes from integrating spirituality and a language of faith into what you say and do. Reliability measures "actions, and how dependable you appear." Actions need to follow words. Do you 'say what you do and do what you say'? People need to know that you will come through for them. Intimacy considers "how safe people feel in sharing with and being with you." So often we are emotionally distant from others, but it is important to create opportunities to ensure that leaders keep their emotional distance from their followers. Likewise, when one is presented with confidential information, they must keep it so. The fourth characteristic, self-orientation, refers to personal focus on both yourself and others.

The equation demonstrates that too much self-focus lowers one's degree of trustworthiness. It is important to demonstrate a strong ego but if your power is all about you, then few will follow. Self-orientation refers to that focus. Self-orientation, which sits alone in the denominator, is thus the most important variable in the Trust Quotient. A person with low self-orientation is free to completely and honestly focus on the other person, not for his own sake, but for the sake of the other person. Thus, lowering self-orientation can improve trustworthiness. When all focus is on helping prospects, their trust of you increases. Ego is a common impediment to learning and the cultivation of talent. With success, it can blind us to our faults and sow future problems. In failure it magnifies each blow and makes recovery more difficult. At every stage, ego holds us back (Holliday 2016). Thus, understanding the Trust Quotient and its attributes can serve as a check on those of us who may think we are trustworthy, but perhaps may not be credible or reliable; or we may be too self-absorbed to notice our deficiency. Building trust is ultimately about people. These attributes point to two pillars of building trust: competence (delivering on promises) and ethical behaviour (doing the right thing and working to improve society). Having a good score for trust requires good 'scores' on all four variables in the Trust Quotient. You want high credibility, reliability and intimacy, and low self-orientation. This equation can be used to determine trust of migrants but also between migrants as well. The meanings are almost entirely personal, not institutional, as people rarely give over their trust to institutions; in effect they trust other people. It is not just in the message that is described as credible and reliable (the first two components of the Trust Quotient) but in the people who deliver the message and who model what that message is. In this sense intimacy and self-orientation are almost entirely about people.

Living the four Trust Values is the best way to increase your trustworthiness. So how would one work to build those 4 trust values? This raises the question; how can we develop trust? This can be done with the 4 Rs of Trust-building (Mohamed Saleem, Forthcoming 2023):

1. Take *Responsibility*

The first concept for ensuring trust and developing credibility is taking personal responsibility and recognising that we individually need to contribute towards the 4 trust attributes. The individual step begins with a values integration to model the change and be a catalyst for the change we want to see. Change comes from taking courage to challenge the status quo and those that perpetuate fear and distrust. *Taking responsibility* is not just for the select few but for everyone to step forward to take the lead in overcoming division.

Taking personal responsibility also means moving *beyond victimhood* to overcome burdens that can destroy in order to give a new lease of life. The historian Yuval Harari has explained that the shift of human beings from small family social units to nations and ideologies gathering millions owes a great deal to our ability to invent and then believe in stories (Harari 2020). In other words, having common "imagined realities" that allow us to believe in invisible constructs as a way of organising ourselves. Hence there is a need to reconstruct the narrative of the community that is one that moves away from victimhood and takes responsibility for addressing social change to address concrete cause-and-effect relations (Harari 2018).

2. Build *Relationships*

How can we expect the people we serve to trust us, if we are not willing to trust them? How can we trust them if there is no engagement? The second pillar is thus about engagement and outreach. Studies conducted in Sri Lanka after the end of the conflict between by the Asian Foundation, found that there was mistrust between the various faith groups largely because there was no day-to-day engagement between members of their respective communities (The Asia Foundation 2011). Thus, building trust must be about reaching out to the Other to include and listen to everyone, and to dispel misinformation now infinitely magnified and exaggerated in the Internet age. The intention must be dialogue with the aims of understanding, respect, and acceptance. A 2018 Pew Research showed that in Western Europe, familiarity with Muslims was linked to positive views of Muslims and Islam (Gardener and Evans 2018). The emphasis is that personally knowing a Muslim is associated with these positive feelings, not simply knowing something about Islam. This complements the anxious middle theory around refugees. Thus, it all starts with getting to know the other. In some cases, it is about breaking bread or having a cup of tea with the other. It is about getting to know the Other, to learn about their culture and traditions, and to share a meal with them. This requires the practice of humility because it involves listening to what they have to say. This is true community engagement. We all need to do more to build those bridges and relationships. There is no magic formula to build those bridges rather, one must be humble with an ability to listen, build relationships with diverse communities, and be willing to learn from and understand others. Building relationships is hence about dialogue.

3. Ensure *Respect*

Building relationships is about ensuring respect for others. One of the key components is to ensure a space for dialogue that is safe is built where what is discussed is not only kept confidential, but more importantly that the spaces are welcoming. For example, if there is a need to build trust with religious leaders or representatives from other faiths, one should not shy away from integrating an intentional space for prayer or other rituals. By allowing for this, it does not diminish one's belief but allows respect to be maintained. Providing space for religious actors to utilise their religious rituals and sacred texts will enhance the comprehension, motivation, or application of the programme in their communities (Abu-Nimer 2018). Respect is also about doing what you say and following through. We need to be honest about what can be done and not done, which includes following through on promises.

4. Always *Reflect*

Self-reflection and self-assessment are very important for understanding where you might go wrong and for acknowledging the past so that you can learn from it. Trust should not be second to accountability. It's not good enough to say, "Trust us." It's not only about corruption, political influence, paternalism, and hypocrisy even though there need to be checks and balances in place that are visibly functioning and give people a reason to trust you. If you want to reduce your self-interest, you need to put a check on those human and organisational tendencies. This requires self-reflection and humble correction. This is where dialogue and trust are mutually reinforcing.

Network for Dialogue – facilitators of refugee and migrant's integration experience

The Network for Dialogue was established in 2019 by the International Dialogue Center KAICIID as a pan-European platform of faith-based and civil society actors working on the social inclusion of refugees and migrants in Europe. One of the distinguishing elements in comparison to already existing networks is the use of intercultural and interreligious dialogue in the grassroots work of its members. This unique approach is applied in smaller or larger scale projects with refugees and migrants with a focus on social cohesion, humanitarian work, supporting education and countering hate-speech. In the period of 2.5 years, Network grew to 25 members and 15 countries with a mixture of faith and civil society representatives. Network was established as a platform to support mutual learning and sharing experiences, joint action in different countries across Europe, and to provide recommendations for policy-makers based on bottom-up experiences.

Research methodology included semi-structured interviews with Network members who identify themselves to be faith-based with the focus on the following thematic areas:

> Motivating factors to get involved in the work with refugees and migrants

> Uniqueness in the approach

> Challenges faced in the grassroots work

> What worked in practice

The examples from faith-based organisations from the Network for Dialogue analysed in this paper, indicate some of the possible ways dialogue can be used at the grassroots level to support social inclusion of refugees and migrants. The research showed that faith-based organisations have an important role in the migration support system across Europe and that they approach humanitarian work in their own particular ways. By using dialogue in their work, representatives of faith-based organisations underline two key elements in creating space for inclusion: overcoming stereotypes by using interreligious and intercultural dialogue and building trust through personal relationships. In the grassroots work of faith-based organizations included in the research, dialogue is seen as "an effective approach to strengthen social cohesion within culturally and religiously diverse societies because which allows for people to maintain their various identities while still finding common ground."[6] In the research study on FBOs in Serbia, it is

---

[6]   https://www.kaiciid.org/publications-resources/project-integration-through-dialogue-toolkit-handbook (accessed 01 February 2022)

underlined that "in addition to directly helping migrants and supporting the official reception system governed by the state, faith-based organisations play a role at the social level. Their perceived major success lies in linking local communities and migrants through joint activities" (Stojic Mitrovic, Djuric Milovanovic 2017: 222). Lyck-Bowen and Owen argue that "Many FBOs have a long-standing tradition of being able to mobilise resources and networks for a wide variety of altruistic activities, ranging from local, social and community work, to help deliver humanitarian aid and disaster relief in countries around the world. However, although religious organisations have long been involved in positively contributing to integration processes, they have traditionally tended to work alongside each other, and less often have organisations from different religious and faith traditions collaborated. More recently, cooperation between religious groups and traditions has become increasingly common, and this study explores what might be termed as a 'multi-religious approach to integration" (Lyck-Bowen, Own, 2019: 22).

In Italy, Network for Dialogue member ADRA – Adventist Relief and Development Agency, works with various groups including refugees and migrants. The motto of ADRA is "to serve humanity so all may live as God intended." ADRA Italy director, Dag Pontvik underlines that:

> [W]e are hoping to bring back the value of the person. Refugees and migrants are in those groups. ADRA hopes to support, give hope and be close to these people. We have a special Sabbath for refugees every year across the world. Trying to join our forces and serve God supporting those in need. The Bible says, in Deuteronomy 10:19 'So you also must love the foreigner, since you yourselves were foreigners in the land of Egypt.' This means, God looks on refugees as equal. Everybody is deserving the love of God. Grace and love and caring for people are core in the work we are doing. Respecting the faith of the person.

The efforts of people working in faith-based organisations can be understood as "facilitators of integration experience." Especially in transit countries, providing continuity and long-term support are some of the most demanding tasks for faith-based organisations, often making their work unpredictable and hard to plan. As Dag Pontvik confirms from transit country experience, "You cannot resolve the journey of the people, you would like but they are not going to stay. The biggest challenge is lack of continuity. Italy is often just a transit country. They don't want to stay here. They are asking: 'What can you give me? Money to send back home?'"[7]

Similar transit countries challenge experienced Network member from Serbia – JRS (Jesuit Refugee Service). In May 2017, the Jesuit Refugee Service (JRS) in Serbia started providing safe accommodation for unaccompanied minors in Belgrade. Before creating this shelter, separated and unaccompanied minors used to stay in refugee camps with adults without having any kind of protection or support. The JRS created the Integration House where unaccompanied refugees and separated children are offered a safe shelter and benefit from education along with health and psychosocial support. Unaccompanied minors and separated children may often be victims of human trafficking, domestic or war violence, sexual, physical, verbal or other abuse.

The Network member, God's House, from Sweden, is an example of a dialogue initiative that started as an interfaith exchange between Muslims and Catholics. In Fisksätra near Stockholm, God's House organises lectures, social work activities, dialogue projects, peace prayers and other activities depending on the needs of the community. In the activities focused on refugees who are coming from various cultural and religious backgrounds, God's House is a space where they feel that they can express themselves freely without any judgments or prejudices. They have created a safe space. Thus, for migrants and refugees one of their first points of call when arriving to this area is the church i.e. God's House. It is a community place to come, to be a bridge between the newcomers and society in general. Along with focus on dialogue, God's House is providing support in finding adequate housing, work, education, satisfaction of basic daily needs and of course spiritual and personal support. Most importantly, God's House represents a safe space and space to develop trust, which can be done if you have a community to be part of. As Rev. Carl Dälback stresses:

> Cultural and ethnic differences can prove a challenge when dealing with such a diverse community, we do our best to make all that come to us feel respected and welcome as they are, in their beliefs and cultures. The language barrier is also another issue that can present a challenge to our work, to facilitate that work we have built a multi-cultural, multi-language team that is fluent in a dozen languages. The lack of basic knowledge of the Swedish society that

[7] Interview with Dag Pontvik, June 2021.

some of our visitors show is also a challenge. Stockholm is one of the most opportunity rich cities in Europe to those who can express themselves, for those who know how the authorities work, how the system functions, one future path is advancing our guests capacity in this respect. We have struggle to connect with Muslim women and motivate them to participate.[8]

Concluding remarks

In addressing the concerns of the anxious middle facing migration in Europe, FBOs, Religious Institutions, and Religious Leaders are increasingly bridges to and points of connection between local communities and migrants. This is true of the nature of work that faith organisations do during times of disasters, where all faiths, however different theologically, have a common purpose to serve humanity and aid the disadvantaged. Religious institutions and actors can offer cultural, social, and political networks unsurpassed by any other (Saleem and Hovey 2014). This is the advantage borne out by engaging with faith institutions, as is seen in the example of the Network for Dialogue. Faith leaders provide spiritual capital and an ability to speak a common language. FBOs can provide a safe and space for conversation but this is strengthened through the dialogical process, which is also part of building trust between each other. Interreligious and intercultural dialogue create opportunities to humanise the Other.

Stressing the key role of interreligious and intercultural dialogue in daily work of faith-based organisations from the Network for Dialogue, its members aim to achieve a better understanding of culturally and religiously sensitive questions related to the social inclusion and integration of refugees and migrants in Europe. This includes having a better awareness and literacy about the different faiths of people who are displaced. For many of them, the lived experience of faith is important as an anchor point between their past and present. It gives them a sense of stability amidst flux. However, there can be a clash with their cultural views and worldviews and between those of the country hosting them. Often this is based on stereotypes and negative perceptions from misinformation. Thus, there is a need to create a space to address this. Through its innovative and dynamic approach, the Network offers new perspectives of dialogical approaches, religiously or culturally, that could be used by newcomers and organizations working with refugees and

---

[8] Interview with Rev. Carl Dälback in June 2021.

migrants to help them face less exclusion and to be better aware of the new cultural and religious environment of the host community. This is done by creating safe spaces for dialogue and by building trust through mutual engagement. Building those relationships is vital to ensuring greater understanding and establishing trust through dialogue. The Network, through its dialogue practices, helps in facing stereotypes, prejudices and misconceptions related to the different Other. The experience of the Network for Dialogue shows us the role of dialogue to build trust that creates the ideas and institutions that will allow us to live together as the global tribe. Thus, the Network is an example of creating a safe space for critical self-reflection that allows one to reach out to treat the other with respect and to enables communities to move towards a common good of peaceful existence with each other.

The famous Victorian explorer Sir Richard Burton[9] once wrote that "All Faith is false; all Faith is true: Truth is the shattered mirror strown in myriad bits; while each believes his little bit the whole to own" *(The Kasidah of Haji Abdu El-Yezdi)*. In his mind, he meant that one finds parts of the truth everywhere and the whole truth nowhere. This concept of the 'shattered mirror concept' enables us to see that "each shard reflects one part of a complex truth from its own particular angle" (Appiah 2006).

Distrust comes from the fact that we consider that "our little shard can reflect the whole" and that our little truth is the whole truth. Building trust is about understanding that for the common good,

each of us (with our faith and spiritual teachings) have a bit of that shard of broken glass. These small sherds of glass which, require careful positioning to create a compelling mosaic that will allow us to live together as the global tribe we have become. Trust building starts with us as individuals and grows with the communities in which we live and work. This is what Network for Dialogue highlights.

References

Abrams, Douglas. 2010. "Processes of prejudice: Theory, evidence and intervention", Equality and Human Rights Commission.

Abu-Nimer, Mohammed. 2018. "Alternative Approaches to Transforming Violent Extremism - The Case of Islamic Peace and Interreligious Peacebuilding". In: *Transformative Approaches to Violent Extremism - Berghoff Handbook Dialogue Series*, Beatrix

---

[9] Among other exploits, Burton managed in 1853 to gain entry to Mecca and Median as a pilgrim, helping to communicate the complexity and richness of Islamic culture to Victorian Britain.

Austin and Hans J. Giessmann (eds). Berlin: Berghoff Foundation.

Abu-Nimer, Mohammed, and Renata K. Smith. 2016. "Interreligious and intercultural education for dialogue, peace and social cohesion", *International Review of Education* (Springer) 62 (4): 393-405.

Andrabi, Abroo Aman. 2020. "Interfaith Dialogue:its need, importance, and merits in the contemporary world", *International Journal of Advanced Academic Studies*, 2(3): 264-271.

Appiah, Kwame Anthony. 2006. *Cosmopolitanism: Ethics in a World of Strangers*. New York: W.W. Norton.

Ballinger, Steve, Rutter, Jill, and Katwala, Sunder. 2017. *How to win the argument for refugee protection*. British Future.

British Red Cross. 2019. "Evaluation of the Open Arms Project", British Red Cross

Corcoran, Rob. 2010. *Trustbuilding: An Honest Conversation on Race, Reconciliation and Responsibiity*. University of Virginia Press.

Dempster, Helen, and Hargrave, Karen. 2017. "Understanding Public Attitudes towards Refugees and Migrants". ODI Working Papers

Fiddian-Qasmiyeh, Elena. 2011. "Introduction: Faith-based humanitarianism in context of forced displacement", *Journal of Refugee Studies* 24(3), 429-439.

Fiske, Susan T. 2017. "Prejudices in Cultural Contexts: Shared Stereotypes (Gender, Age) Versus Variable Stereotypes (Race, Ethnicity, Religion)". *Perspect Psychol Sci*. 2017 Sep. 12(5):791-799

Gardener, S., & Evans, J. (2018, 07 24). *In Western Europe, familiarity with Muslims is linked to positive views of Muslims and Islam*. Pew Research Centre: https://www.pewresearch.org/fact-tank/2018/07/24/in-western-europe-familiarity-with-muslims-is-linked-to-positive-views-of-muslims-and-islam/

Hamlin, Rebecca. 2021. "Crossing: How we label and react to people on the move", Stanford University Press

Harari Y. 2018. *21 Lessons for the 21st Century*. Jonathan Cape.

Harari, Y. (2020, Jan 24). *Yuval Harari's blistering warning to Davos*. World Economic Forum. https://www.weforum.org/agenda/2020/01/yuval-hararis-warning-davos-speech-future-predications/

Hawkins, Stephen. 2019. "Speaking to Core Beliefs: Communicating about Immigration in 2019-2020". More in Common

Holliday R. (2016). *Ego is the Enemy*. Penguin.

KAICIID 2021. "Guide to Interreligious Dialogue: Bridging Differences and Building Sustainable Societies", KAICIID Manuals, Vienna

Katwala, Sunder, and Will Somerville. 2016. "Engaging the Anxious Middle on Immigration Reform: Evidence from the UK Debate." *Migration Policy*. May. Accessed January 2021. www.migrationpolicy.org/research/engaging-anxious-middle-immigration-reform-evidence-uk-debate.

Lyck-Bowen, Majbritt, and Mark Owen. 2019. "A Multi-religious response to the migrant crises in Europe: A preliminary examination of potential benefits of multi-religious cooperation on the integration of migrants". *Journal of Ethnic and Migration Studies* 45(1), 21-41.

Maister D. Galford R. Green C. H. 2000. *The Trusted Advisor*. Simon & Schuster.

Mavelli, Luca, and Wilson, Erin (eds.). 2017. *The Refugee Crises and Religion: Secularism, Security and Hospitality in Question*. London, New York: Rowman & Littlefield.

Mohamed-Saleem, Amjad. Forthcoming 2023. "The Challenge of Building Trust Digitally." In Dynamics of Dialogue, Cultural Development, and Peace in the Metaverse". Chakraborty, Swati (ed.), 122-139. Hershey, PA: IGI Global. https://doi.org/10.4018/978-1-6684-5907-2.ch011

Moretti, Sebastian, and Tiziana Bozon. 2017. "Some Reflections on the IFRC's approach to Migration and Displacement". *International Review of the Red Cross* (ICRC) 99 (1): 153-178.

Note, N., Fornet-Betancourt, R., Estermann, J., Aerts, D. 2009. "Worldview and Cultures: Philosophical Reflections from an Intercultural Perspective. An Introduction". In: Note, N., Fornet-Betancout, R., Estermann, J., Aerts, D. (eds.) *Worldviews and Cultures. Einstein Meets Magritte: An Interdisciplinary Reflection on Science, Nature, Art, Human Action and Society*, vol 10. Springer, Dordrecht.

Orton, Andrew. 2012. *Building migrants' belonging through positive interaction*. Strasbourg: Council of Europe. Available at: https://www.coe.int/t/democracy/migration/ Source/migration/EnglishMigrantBelongingWeb.pdf

Saleem, Amjad and Hovey, Guy. 2014 "Faith, relief and development: the UMCOR-Muslim Aid model seven years on", *Forced Migration Review* 48, 33-35.

Sen, Amartya. 2006. *Identity & Violence*. Oxford: Penguin Books.

Stanley, Joe. 2019. "Dear Theophilus: Cultures and Worldviews", https://www.gcu. edu/blog/theology-ministry/dear-theophilus-worldviews-and-cultures

Stojić Mitrović, Marta, and Aleksandra Djurić Milovanović. 2020. "The Humanitarian Enagemenet of faith-based organisations in Serbia: balancing between the vulnerable human and the (in)secure (nation)state", In: *Forced Migration and Human Security in the Eastern Orthodox World*, ed. Lucian N. Leustean. London: Routledge, 207-228.

The Asia Foundation. 2011. National Values Survey 2011, Colombo, Sri Lanka. The Asia Foundation.

"TEXTUAL PLACEMAKING AND MIGRATION MEMORIES IN PSALM 137"

Eric M. Trinka[1]

This chapter arose from an interest in the broader question of how religious texts form and function as catalysts and containers of memory in contexts of mobility and migration. It is well documented by now that religion plays important roles for many migrants throughout the migration undertaking.[2] Religion is embedded in the social world of migration decision-making and informs responses to (in)security.[3] Religious practice also plays an integral role in shaping, perpetuating, and responding to cultures of mobility and migration regimes. Textualized creations are among the mnemonic cultural products mobile/migrant religious actors generate.[4] Some such texts become sacralized for communities of faith and may even as function as foundational resources in later contexts of movement.

The task at hand is to explore how analyses of biblical sources might help answer larger questions about textual creation and placemaking in contexts of migration and exile, specifically, how text-making is a form of religious coping that sustains later generations of migrants. In this essay, I approach such questions with the case study of Psalm 137, a text associated with the Babylonian exile of Judean populations in the 6th century BCE, which was a formative period for the biblical corpus. Beginning in the ancient past is intentional. The Bible, as a resource of faith to which many modern migrants turn, contains numerous migration-related texts that are products of migration experiences and

---

[1] Eric M. Trinka, Emory & Henry College, Virginia, U.S..
[2] Jennifer B. Saunders, Elena Fiddian-Qasmiyeh, and Susanna Snyder, eds. *Intersections of Religion and Migration: Issues at the Global Crossroads* (New York: Palgrave MacMillan, 2016); Elżbieta M. Goździak and Dianna J. Shandy, "Editorial Introduction: Religion and Spirituality in Forced Migration," *Journal of Refugee Studies* 15 (2002): 129-35; Eric M. Trinka, "Migration and Internal Religious Pluralism: A Review of Present Findings," *The Journal of Interreligious Studies* 28 (2019): 3-23.
[3] Jeffery H. Cohen and Ibrahim Sirkeci, *Cultures of Migration: The Global Nature of Contemporary Mobility* (Austin: University of Texas Press, 2011), 1-19.
[4] Jorge Durand and Douglas S. Massey, "Miracles on the Border: The Votive Art of Mexican Migrants to the United States," in *Art in the Lives of Immigrant Communities in the United States*, eds. Paul DiMaggio and Patricia Fernández-Kelly (New Brunswick, NJ: Rutgers University Press, 2010), 214-28, 214-15. See also, Gloria Giffords, *Mexican Folk Retablos: Masterpieces on Tin* (Tucson: University of Arizona Press, 1974); Octavio Solis, *Retablos: Stories from a Life Lived Along the Border* (San Francisco: City Light, 2018); Gabriella Soto, "Migrant *Memento Mori* and the Geography of Risk," *Journal of Social Archaeology* 16 (2016): 335-58.

have been shaped through reception and redaction by authors and audiences who moved for various reasons over the span of their compositional histories.

The biblical corpus' expansive range of text types and content has fostered broad interpretation and application across the millennia of its existence. Among its most drawn upon motifs are those regarding movement and migration. Beyond narratives of human movement, the Bible's pluriform theological perspectives are also present in intertextual conversations regarding divine mobility. On one hand, there are biblical voices that enunciate that Israel and Judah's God is a deity who remains above being eternally tied to a singular geography or location. On the other hand, there are voices demanding that God is forever bound to a particular location through historic acts of covenant-making. The tenor of these differences is apparent in the Judahite experiences of Babylonian relocation, which underpin Psalm 137.

Historical Contexts of Judean Exile

The nature of the ancient sources is such that on one hand biblical stories of migration, mobility, and oppression relate to audiences across a variety of historical contexts. Yet, on the other hand, the same texts obfuscate their contexts of origin and fail to contain specific information about experiences of exile. Thus, scholars look for contemporaneous sources that might inform historical reconstructions of mobility regimes in the world around ancient Israel and the Bible.

Following a period of military conquest and territorial expansion in the 6th century BCE, Babylonian relocations of Judean populations brought peoples from Judah to Mesopotamia. In addition, groups fleeing Babylonian hegemony sought refuge and political support in Egypt and neighboring lands. As part of their incursions in the land of Judah in 587/86, Babylonian forces destroyed much of the city of Jerusalem and its Temple, thus upending the religious lives of many in the city and surrounding region. It was the understanding of many exiled Judeans that Jerusalem was the home of Israel's God, Yahweh, and was therefore inviolable as both sacred and political space. Questions of divine power and presence multiplied as worshipers of Yahweh wrestled with the realities of Babylonian victory. Had they witnessed divine defeat, abandonment, or something else? Destruction of the Temple resulted in drastic changes to worship paradigms and shifting centers of religious power. The experience of exile catalyzed the reworking of established religious texts and creation of new ones, generating an increase in the prominence and pluriformity of textually bound forms of religiosity.

Among contemporary extra-biblical sources from the Babylonian period, several textual archives originating in southern Mesopotamia bear importance for reconstructing Judean experiences of relocation. These archives include the names of descendants of Judeans who were taken captive by Babylonian forces or who relocated by other means to Babylonia. In the texts from *al-Yāhūdu* and those known as the *Murašû* archive, we find mention of more than 200 persons who are identifiably Judean in ancestral heritage. The nature of these sources as records is rather mundane, with most being contractual records of land holding, use, taxation, and marriage. While the texts do not provide detailed accounts of population resettlements, they indirectly give witness to relocation regimes, economic networks, and dimensions of cultural contact and identity negotiations in Babylonian contexts. It is through them that we can discern the degree to which various communities of West Semitic and Judean ancestry became integrated with the Babylonian population.[5]

Babylonia was agriculturally rich in cereal crops and dates grown throughout its riverine landscape, but agrarian lifeways were tenuously sustained against the constant threats of flooding, silting, and salinization. Agricultural production was hard won through extensive irrigation and continual soil maintenance. This generally resource poor region relied on an extensive import economy for timber and fine goods, but also on large populations of laborers who were brought from surrounding lands. As part of its strategy for agricultural production and resource acquisition, Babylon instigated rural resettlement projects whereby populations of foreigners and some native Babylonians were relocated to complete irrigation projects and develop agriculturally useful land. The fall of Jerusalem and movement of Judean populations to Babylonia maps onto this larger historical landscape of hegemonic expansion and agricultural resettlement projects.[6]

Despite the creative influence the period of Babylonian hegemony

[5] Tero Alstola, *Judeans in Babylon: A Study of Deportees in the Sixth and Fifth Centuries BCE* (Leiden: Brill, 2021); Laurie Pearce, "Cuneiform Sources for Judeans in Babylonia in the Neo-Babylonian and Achaemenid Periods: An Overview," *Religion Compass* 10 (2016): 230-43; Cornelia Wunsch, *Judaeans by the Waters of Babylon. New Historical Evidence in Cuneiform Sources from Rural Babylonia, primarily from the Schøyen Collection.* Babylonische Archive 6. (Dresden: ISLET, 2022).
[6] Eric M. Trinka, *Cultures of Mobility, Migration, and Religion in Ancient Israel and Its World* (London: Routledge, 2022), 55-82.

had on biblical composition, few biblical writings speak directly to Judean experiences of exile. Texts such as 2 Kings, Jeremiah, and 2 Chronicles provide terse accounts of invasions by the Babylonian army, their destructive activities in Judah, and the relocation of various sectors of the population, yet lack detailed information on the processes or endpoints of movement. Lamentations records the carnage of Babylonian siege tactics and the aftermath of Jerusalem's destruction, but we again find little information regarding the specifics of the exiled population's movement or experiences of resettlement. Texts such as Daniel and the Joseph narrative in Genesis deal with questions of acculturation in the contexts of foreign courts, but neither is a reliable source of information regarding the daily lives of Judeans in Babylon.

Rather than including extensive historical chronicles of exile, biblical authors wrestle with the realities of displacement through indirect attestation and analysis that take the form of ancestral origin myths, historiographical epics cataloguing divine intervention to grant freedom from imperial oppression and enslavement, numerous instances of poetic discourse on the nature of divine justice, and stories of righteous persons negotiating religious tensions and ethnic identity in foreign contexts. Such texts deal with core questions of personhood and theology in contexts of migration and relocation by placing the experience of Israel and Judah's ancestors into an omni-temporal conversation with present and future movers. It is no wonder that migrants across time have turned to biblical texts to navigate questions of acculturation and religious identity in contexts of mobility. One can see how subsequent audiences might overlay the motifs of divinely ordained movement, whether as punishment or as restoration, on their own journeys.

Prophetic texts like Ezekiel, Jeremiah, and Isaiah also invite omni-temporal engagement but are still of limited historical use concerning the exile. With complicated and overlapping compositional trajectories, each text provides a unique perspective on the causes of Judean exile. Ezekiel follows the experience of a religious specialist in Babylonian territory most closely. While Jeremiah's visions of exile unfold according to a Jerusalem-centric view that looks to the east, Ezekiel's perspective is from the east with a gaze to the west. Both Ezekiel and Isaiah present understandings of divine presence and mobility that stand in contrast with Jeremiah. In its account of the Babylonian invasion, Ezekiel envisions the Divine Presence abandoning its seat in the Temple and traveling into exile before later returning to Jerusalem and dwelling there forever (Ezekiel 1-10, 43). Isaiah similarly describes the return of the remnant of Judah as a second Exodus, led by none other than Yahweh, who has traveled to Babylon to rescue his people (Isaiah 40-45). Much authorial energy in these prophetic texts is spent delimiting proper religious practice and belief for their audiences. The particular demands for orthopraxis vary among the authors but each shares the understanding that Judah's downfall is related to cultic disobedience. The questions of divine justice and human agency that form the backbone of the prophetic trio represent timeless questions that emerge from the human condition. Collectively, these prophetic narratives center the divine as the prime catalyst of migration, and in doing so, demonstrate a spectrum of theological and practical elasticity in response to human movement.

One text stands out among those briefly surveyed above: Psalm 137. It is in this poem situated in Israel's liturgical collection that we find a description of day-to-day life of persons "on the street" in exile. We turn now to a reading of the psalm in light of studies of memory and placemaking in the context of migration.

Psalm 137 as Site and Cipher of Migrational Memory

Movement and migration are not necessarily traumatic experiences, but the collective memories of destruction and displacement presented in Psalm 137 convey a context of deep suffering in a foreign land. Unique among other texts found in the Psalter, this poem transmits memories of Judeans in Babylonia who contend with past traumas while longing for their ancestral homeland.

1 By the rivers (irrigation canals)[7] of Babylon—

there we sat down and there we wept

when we remembered Zion (Jerusalem).

2 On the willows there

we hung up our harps.

---

[7] The traditional translation of the Hebrew term *nahar* as river in the context of the Psalm obfuscates the more likely reality that the setting for this poem is not the Tigris or Euphrates proper but one of the many irrigation canals constructed along their banks to redirect water through the agricultural lands that stretched into the Babylonian countryside. This translation was first suggested by John J. Ahn in *Exile as Forced Migration: A Sociological, Literary, and Theological Approach on the Displacement and Resettlement of the Southern Kingdom of Judah* (Berlin: de Gruyter, 2011).

³ For there our captors

asked us for songs,

and our tormentors asked for mirth, saying,

"Sing us one of the songs of Zion!"

⁴ How could we sing the Lord's song

in a foreign land?

⁵ If I forget you, O Jerusalem,

let my right-hand wither!

⁶ Let my tongue cling to the roof of my mouth,

if I do not remember you,

if I do not set Jerusalem

above my highest joy.

⁷ Remember, O Lord, against the Edomites

the day of Jerusalem's fall,

how they said, "Tear it down! Tear it down!

Down to its foundations!"

⁸ O daughter Babylon, you devastator!

Happy shall they be who pay you back

what you have done to us!

⁹ Happy shall they be who take your little ones

and dash them against the rock!

* Translation New Revised Standard Version. Parenthetical additions are author's own.

Biblical scholars have broadly agreed that the Psalm's provenance should be located during the period of Babylonian captivity.[8] If so, the poem was likely composed after the initial translocation to Babylonia. It is, however, possible that the origin of the poem lies in a time after the return of some community members to Yehud (formerly Judah) following the Persian defeat of Babylon in the 6th century. Biblical scholars interested in situating Psalm 137 in the broader context of the book of Psalms have categorized the poem according to different sub-

---

[8] Ahn, *Exile as Forced Migration*, 77-78.

genres. While clarifying genre is integral to interpreting a literary creation, for the purpose of this essay, the categorical boundaries of the poem as a Psalm of Lament or Zion Psalm are less important than trying to understand the broader function of poetry as an act of textual placemaking and a collective response to cultural trauma. It is noteworthy, as Ahn recognizes, that in its final place in the biblical corpus, Psalm 137 is located between Hallelujah and Thanksgiving Psalms.[9] The outcome of this is that the pslam can simultaneously be read as conforming to these other poems of praise and gratitude while offering a purposeful juxtaposition to them. Regardless of the date or place of authorship, the psalm preserves the collective memory of Judean laborers in a moment of pause on the banks of a canal (re)construction project. There, they are taunted by Babylonian overseers who demand from them a joyful song about their destroyed homeland.

Memory, which is often understood as emplaced and analyzed through the cipher of stasis, is as dynamic in form and meaning as place. The stories composing our daily existence represent the fluidity of social life, which is essentially mobile.[10] In line with Doreen Massey, we acknowledge that place is constituted partially through narrative accumulation.[11] What studies of memory and movement demonstrate is that memory develops through movement and is paradoxically situated in a matrix of mobile experiences. Julia Creet helps us consider the agglomerative nature of memory as containing the past but ultimately existing as a collection of experiences and interpretations manifest in the present. Thus, "Memory is where we have arrived rather than where we have left."[12] In the larger matrix of textually bound religiosities, narratives of Israel and Judah's origins and of their ancestors' experiences of movement and captivity came to form sites of engagement and re-enactment that placed recipients of the texts squarely in the middle of the migratory journeys told within the texts. Psalm 137 represents the personal trauma of those tormented along the banks of the Babylonian canals and the collective cultural trauma that those singular events represent in synecdochic fashion not only for members of the exilic populations but also for subsequent generations who count the exile's

---

[9] Ahn, *Exile as Forced Migration*, 81-82.

[10] John Urry, *Sociology Beyond Society*, (London: Routledge, 2000), 1-20.

[11] Doreen Massey, *For Space* (London: Sage, 2005), 12-13.

[12] Julia Creet, "The Migration of Memories and Memories of Migration," in *Memory and Migration: Multidisciplinary Approaches to Memory Studies*, eds. Julia Creet and Andreas Kitzmann (Toronto: University of Toronto Press, 2011), 3-26, 6.

experience as part of their ancestral story or claim it as their own.[13] Hearers of the psalm enter into it, envisioning themselves on the banks of the canals with their ancestors regardless of temporal or geographic distance that separates them.

Poetry is but one creative facet of language that can be marshaled in response to trauma. Myriad studies have documented the power of poetry as a critical and constructive tool migrants employ to process mundane movement and traumatic upheavals, negotiate cultural differences and challenges, bolster emotional resilience, create place, and construct meaning.[14] Imagination is the wellspring of hope, but it is often one of the first aspects of personhood immobilized by trauma. Modern studies of traumatized persons have identified one of the widespread effects of trauma as stunted imaginative capacity.[15] Perhaps such an observation reads as an innocuous aftereffect of trauma but consider the deprivation one experiences in all aspects of their life with limited capabilities for imagining. Victims often oscillate between numbness and rage, locked in a cycle of past trauma and present triggers, incapable of entering the imaginative space to see or feel beyond the event or circumstances in which they caused or experience physical or moral injury.

The power of poetry is such that it provides means to reconstruct imaginative pathways in the brain. Poetry often encourages us to see the newness of that which is familiar to us through subversive presentation of linguistic and syntactical norms. Poets often bend aspects of linguistic normativity to guide their audiences in seeing the world anew. Whether by throwing light on the mundane aspects of existence or through pulling the sheet out from under our assumptions of what is true, right, and beautiful, poets reveal to us the parts of life that frequently escape our view. The purposeful distillation of thought and experience that produces poetry through atomization and reconcentration mirrors the fracturing and reconstitution of community that migrants can experience in the process of relocation, particularly those who move with restricted agency.

[13] David W. Stowe, *Song of Exile: The Enduring Mystery of Psalm 137* (New York: Oxford University Press, 2016).

[14] Maghiel van Crevel, "Debts: Coming to Terms with Migrant Worker Poetry," *Chinese Literature Today* 8 (2019): 127-45; Sanghamitra Dalal, "Locating Diasporic Interspaces of Local Modernities: Malaysian Migrant Poetry Competition and Voices of the Displaced," *Journal of Literature, Culture and Literary Translation* 1.12 (2021): 1-23; Darrel Alejandro Holnes "Migrant Psalms: Poems" (Evanston: Northwestern University Press, 2021).

15 Bessel van der Kolk, *The Body Keeps the Score: Brain, Mind, and Body in the Healing of Trauma* (New York: Penguin, 2014), 51-73.

The idiom of poetic discourse forms a response to the past but also a window on the present.

Religious idioms, in the forms of language and praxis, accomplish more than sense-making. They are elements by which the very worlds we inhabit are constructed.[16] Psalm 137 is not simply an epithet for a bygone city, or a lament of lives lost but rather a textual landscape that offers readers an opportunity to engage in subversive poetic placemaking. As the Psalmist recounts Jerusalem's destruction, both humans and God are called to action. The psalm plays on the themes of forced labor and recreation, and by its recitation, leads the audience to see themselves into it to participate in a process of re-creation of place and community. The places of the irrigation canals, Babylon, Zion, and Edom named in Psalm 137 are not static representations of location but dynamic and comprehensive sites of memory. The synonymous use of locative terminology for historical memory (i.e. "there" also meaning "then"), demonstrates the ways place and time overlap in the process of memory. For example, in vv. 1-2, the term "there" (שָׁם) functions as a locative stand-in for the irrigation canals and Babylonia writ large but also for the "then" of the period of exile. If the poem's origin is in Babylon, the use of "there" may act to distinguish the place of torment from the "here" of the compositional landscape somewhere beyond the canals but still in exile. If, the point of origin is beyond Babylon, "there" stands in contrast to the "here" of a temporal or spatial point later in the migrational trajectory. The effect of the comparison is that the unspoken "here" of the psalm's author, wherever they are when it is uttered, is contained within the "there." That is to say, there is no present place or time that is not inflected by the "there" of the psalm's collective memory.

The psalmist recounts the Babylonian tormentors (תּוֹלָלֵינוּ) demands for a joyful song—poetry put in musical form—from the Judeans, while the audience wonders along with the migrant workers, "How could we sing the LORD's (Yahweh's) song in a foreign land?" We pause to ponder the place-bound essence of Judah's poetic discourse with its God in the Jerusalem Temple and the potential for that discourse to be halted when members of the community are removed from their home after witnessing the destruction of their Temple. We also contemplate the complicated realities of a future the Psalmist may not know, whereby some of Judean ancestry returned to their homeland while a majority

---

[16] Robert A. Orsi, "Everyday Miracles: The Study of Lived Religion," in *Lived Religions in America: Toward a History of Practice*, ed. David D. Hall (Princeton: Princeton University Press, 1997), 3-21.

opted to remain in Babylon under Persian control. We wonder how those in diaspora understood themselves in relation to this poem.

While the initial response to the Babylonian's demand for a song is a declaration of impossibility given the grievous separation from homeland and sacred geography, the subsequent retort demonstrates that singing is precisely the way the Judean migrants might constructively engage an imbalance of power and cry out for justice in the very presence of the Babylonians who demand a display of mirth. By recalling Zion, another name for Jerusalem, they bring the destroyed city back into mnemonic existence in a new land. The Psalmist's thus demonstrates the very power of poetic remembrance as an act of spatial transference, chronological confluence, and communal reconstitution wherein through recollection as reenactment, the audience is invited to participate in the collective (re)constitution of the self and the identity of the group, wherever they are. Jerusalem may be destroyed, but it can exist in heart, and in mind, and even in practice far away across space and time. In this context, to sing is an act of subversive religious coping. It is corporate singing, after all, that forms part of the ritual repertoire of activities at the Jerusalem Temple. The implication is that the community can sing their memories of Jerusalem and thus recreate its essentials elements, namely their relationship with the Divine and the community of faith. Thus, verses 4-6 sound a warning to not allow Jerusalem slip away into the past. If one allows themselves to forget, these verses demand that they should suffer the inability to ever sing or play an instrument again.

The psalm turns from intentions of remembrance and reconstruction to recollections of neighborly backstabbing by the Edomites, Judah's ancestral kin to the east. As the Judeans lament the horrific death of their innocent young ones at the hands of their enemies, they besiege God to repay the perpetrators in kind. Thus, the "song of mirth" ends on a subversively gruesome note of infanticide. What might it mean to imagine such violence? Perhaps the memories of retributive destruction and infanticide in Psalm 137 demonstrate that the author of this poem has not fully assimilated their own trauma of witnessing lives so needlessly and violently ended, lost lives that represent in perpetuity stunted future generations. Such a demands for retributive justice seems to only make sense in a context of profound power imbalance where the victims of violence seek an unobtainable resolution. Joerstad has remarked that the unsavory ending of Psalm 137 can catalyze a process of ethical reflection by which readers are sensitized to the violence of colonialist regimes of population control and land acquisition.[17] Still, the psalm ends on the starting line for a new cycle of violence. Part of the dark comedy of Psalm 137 is that the Psalmist likely intends readers to envision a situation in which the Babylonian tormentors know little or no Hebrew. Thus, the Judeans are free to sing songs of their homeland that call for the destruction of their enemies in the very presence of their enemies(!)

It may be tempting to read this psalm and to dismiss it on one level as the product of an overactive religious imagination. We might assume, after all, that places cannot change location or that the divine does not interject in human affairs. But to suggest either of these things may belie our own post-Enlightenment social scientific outlooks on the world. Worse yet, acting on such assumptions would demonstrate that we are failing to take seriously the roles that religion or religious texts play in the lives of many migrants.

Psalm 137 catalyzes powerful personal and collective memories that later readers have seen themselves into in myriad ways.[18] The propensity of readers to locate themselves as observers or participants in religious texts is a phenomenon first explored according to the rubrics of modern psychological study by Hjalmar Sundén.[19] Sundén's work was focused on moments of crisis among Christian adherents who came to understand their life experiences through personal identification with biblical texts or characters. The practitioners observed by Sundèn viewed their experience as being integrated in religious meta-narratives, and even more specifically as part of a divinely sanctioned plan. Important correctives have been leveled against Sundèn's approach, but theories of "role-taking" remain salient.[20] Scholars have not dismissed Sundén's application of role theory to biblical texts wholesale but have expanded the theoretical grounds from which it is applied. Narrative psychology has also offered important complementary approaches to Sundén's theoretical framework by grounding the narrative tendencies present across history in the scientific study of human development, cognition,

---

[17] Mari Joerstad, "Sing Us the Songs of Zion: Land Culture, and Resistance in Psalm 137, *12 Years a Slave* and *Cedar Man*," *Horizons in Biblical Theology* 40 (2018): 1-16.

[18] Emily Keightley and Michael Pickering, *The Mnemonic Imagination: Remembering as Creative Practice* (New York: Palgrave Macmillan, 2012), 17.

[19] Hjalmar Sundén *Die Religion und die Rollen* (Berlin: Alfred Töpelmann, 1966); Cf. T. Lindgren, Hjalmar Sundén's Impact on the Study of Religion in the Nordic Countries," *Temenos* 50 (2014): 39-61.

[20] Neal Krause & Kenneth I. Pargament, "Reading the Bible, Stressful Life Events and Hope: Assessing an Overlooked Coping Resource," *Journal of Religion and Health* (2018): 1428-39; Jill B. Hamilton, Angelo D. Moore, Khishanna A. Johnson, and Harold G. Koenig, "Reading the Bible for Guidance, Comfort, and Strength during Stressful Life Events," *Nursing Research* 62 (2013): 178-84.

interaction, and identity creation.[21]

Scholars of migration past and present have much to learn from the psychological study of narrative self-association as an aspect of collective memory. Among the resource sets of migrants past and present, religious narratives hold importance alongside economic and social capital, often providing the means to interpret aspects of mobility understood to be more tangible. Self-association with religious narratives can therefore be categorized coping response to both mundane and traumatic contexts encountered by migrants. Identifying one's experience with religious narratives can take the form of direct character association whereby a person identifies with portrayals of migratory persons in the narrative. While intensely personal, role taking is also part of broader collective interpretive discourse that forms a narrative well from which later generations draw as they formulate their own responses to contexts of mobility and migration.

One's identity as a migrant can be informed by their perceived social location within the historical narrative(s) of their faith. Collective memories of migration, such as Psalm 137, draw from the wells of ancient traditions to facilitate imaginative reasoning and give migrants ways to cope with difficulties and to envision or enact their own successes. Psalm 137 enjoys a profoundly rich history of reception and interpretation in migrational contexts.[22] Narrative has been an essential element of placemaking from the earliest of times. Our daily lives are premised on stories, constructed, and reconstructed through telling and by living them out. In the contexts of mobility and migration, movers must actively negotiate and construct new spaces in environments that often lack stable social networks or familiar cultural elements.[23] Narratives might contain shared memories of religious attachment to particular places or landscapes and make possible the overlay of such attachments on new places. Religious narratives provide means for migrants to actively engage their experiences through identity negotiation, repeating religious histories of movement, reimaging or recreating sites of religious importance, self-identification with key narrative personas, and through

---

[21] Jacob A. Belzen, "On Religious Experience: Role Theory and Contemporary Narrative Psychology," in *Sundén's Role Theory – an Impetus to Contemporary Psychology of Religion*, Nils G. Holm & Jacob A. Belzen, eds.(Åbo: Åbo Akademi, 1995), 47-76; "Beyond a Classic? Hjalmar Sundén's Role Theory and Contemporary Narrative Psychology," *The International Journal for The Psychology of Religion* 6 (1996): 181-99.
[22] Ron Eyerman, *Memory, Trauma, and Identity* (Cham: Palgrave Macmillan, 2019), 29.
[23] Paolo Boccagni, *Migration and the Search for Home* (New York: Palgrave Macmillan, 2017); Manuel A. Vásquez and Kim Knott, "Three Dimensions of Religious Place Making in Diaspora." *Global Networks* 14 (2017): 326-347.

emplacement in their own narrative trajectories.

The contents of memory, both migrational and other, are marked by fluidity of recall. What we remember and how we remember it changes with experience, as our cumulative sense of self grows across time. We remember as persons, embedded in networks of social relationships and identity. Our memories are conditioned by the constraints of context and constructed via the dialectic of individual agency and collective creativity.[24] We see such patterns of recall, reenactment, and negotiation at play as migrants engage the textual corpora of their religious traditions. Biblical scholar, Jacqueline Hidalgo thus describes the Bible as a 'homing device' and 'language world' for migrants as textual moments are reenacted and applied in the present.[25] For example, Liberian migrants residing in Minnesota arrive at the understanding that their own journeys recall, and perhaps even mirror, Joseph's experience in Genesis 37, 39-50. In doing so, they interpret their own movement and acculturation in light of Joseph's suffering and redemption and mapping their experiential trajectory onto a larger divine plan for redemption and restoration.[26] The phenomenon of role-taking is not limited to Jewish or Christian scriptures. Maria Kanal has shown how the Qur'an, *hadith*, and *sunnah* provide sacred resources of narrative engagement for Syrian Muslim migrant women in Turkey.[27] Such processes of continual reinterpretation and reenactment elide the "experience that is being remembered and the experience of remembering." [28]

Conclusion

The biblical corpus' expansive range of text types and content has fostered broad interpretation and application across the millennia of its existence. Within this textual landscape, the Hebrew Bible is famously polyvocal in terms of both genre and theological perspective. The pluriformity of the textual tradition is due in part to trajectories of

---

[24] Keightley and Pickering, *The Mnemonic Imagination*, 18-21.

[25] Jacqueline M. Hidalgo, "The Bible as Homing Device Among Cubans at Claremont's Calvary Chapel," in *Latinxs, the Bible, and Migration*, eds. Efraín Agosto and Jacqueline M. Hidalgo (New York: Palgrave Macmillan, 2018), 21-42, 22, 28.

[26] Frieder Ludwig, "'Just Like Joseph in the Bible': The Liberian Christian Presence in Minnesota." In *African Christian Presence in the West: New Immigrant Congregations and Transnational Networks in North America and Europe*, eds. Frieder Ludwig and J.K. Asamoah-Gyadu Trenton: Africa World Press, 2011), 357-80.

[27] Maria Kanal, "Exploring Coping Strategies of Urban Refugee Women in Iskenderun, Turkey." Presentation given at The Migration Conference, Bari, IT June 18-20, 2019; "The Role of Religion and Culture in the Coping Process of Syrian Refugee Women in Turkey." Presentation given at The Respond Project Conference: Unpacking the Challenges & Possibilities for Migration Governance." University of Cambridge, October 17-19, 2019.

[28] Keightley and Pickering, *The Mnemonic Imagination*, 34-35.

composition, redaction, and canonization that span almost 1000 years. The scribes responsible for the biblical canon are members of an intellectual elite, who among other things had the capacity to mediate the meaning of cultural trauma to their audiences. One might assume then that the scribal tradents of biblical texts would seek to present events of physical and cultural trauma with narrative and theological uniformity. Yet, biblical texts—as a record of revelatory experience and speech—maintain a sense of comprehensiveness that exceeds coherence.[29] One example of this revelatory comprehensiveness can be seen in the textual accounts of Israel and Judah's prophets, who offer competing and complementary interpretations of exilic cultural trauma. As "carrier groups,"[30] prophets disseminate information and codify the content of past events while promoting sanctioned responses to them.

The foregoing study of Psalm 137 demonstrates one biblical perspective on displacement. In its poetic terseness, Psalm 137 prescribes a necessarily selective memory of events. Whether the experience of suffering documented in the psalm were normative for all exiles is not substantiated by the biblical corpus. Extrabiblical evidence attests to relocated populations living and working among the canal networks in a land-grant agricultural system where canal maintenance was a central aspect of labor alongside staple crop production. Whether the contexts described in Psalm 137 were ubiquitously experienced by all Judeans in Babylonia is irrelevant because the aim of the Psalm is such that the memory it preserves became the authoritative account of the past.[31]

Just as the psalm illustrates past events, it offers hope that loss and suffering are cordoned to earlier days. Insomuch, it stands as a resource for those who have suffered along with, or in ways like those in Babylonia. Absent the land, the psalm served as a source of imaginative engagement with the city of Jerusalem and Judah, and with the covenant promises and ideals of divine protection associated with Zion. Upon return to the land, with things once lost now returning—albeit in reformulated ways—the psalm stood as a reminder of where the returned Judeans had once been, physically, theologically, and metaphorically. In this latter sense, Psalm 137 became a complimentary text to Exodus 12; 20; 23:9 and Deuteronomy 5-6 which were fundamental in the self-

---

[29] Sanders article.
[30] Eyerman, *Memory, Trauma, and Identity*, 47.
[31] Irial Glynn and J. Olaf Kleist, "The Memory and Migration Nexus: An Overview," in *History, Memory, and Migration: Perceptions of the Past and the Politics of Incorporation* (London: Palgrave Macmillan, 2012), 3-29.

understanding of later Jewish adherents for their dual role as collective memories of enslavement in Egypt and freedom from oppression. Those later generations who count themselves as having once been slaves in Egypt can in the same way collectively memorialized their captivity in Babylonia. It is this process of commemorative reenactment that likely leads Psalm 137 to be enshrined in Judah's Bible as part of in its liturgical tradition. Later communities who adopted the texts of the biblical corpus as their own came to see themselves within the text in similarly pluriform ways across two millennia.